Sign at the junction of Route 6N and Hill Street, placed through the cooperation of the New York State Department of Education, the Division of Highways, the Enoch Crosby Chapter of the Daughters of the American Revolution, and the American Scenic and Historic Preservation Society.

# SYBIL LUDINGTON

# The Call to Arms

by V. T. Dacquino

**PURPLE MOUNTAIN PRESS**
Fleischmanns, New York

To my parents who taught me love.
To June, Januarie, and Vinny for giving me all the love I need.

*Sybil Ludington: The Call to Arms*
First edition 2000

Published by
PURPLE MOUNTAIN PRESS, LTD.
P.O. Box 309, Fleischmanns, New York 12430-0309
914-254-4062, 914-254-4476 (fax), purple@catskill.net
http://www.catskill.net/purple

Photographs by the author

ISBN 1-930098-09-X

Library of Congress Catalog Card Number:
00-090837

5  4  3  2  1

Manufactured in the United States of America on acid-free paper.

# Table of Contents

On March 25, 1975, the Daughters of the American Revolution, in collaboration with the United States Postal Service, held a ceremony in Carmel, New York, to celebrate the first-day issue of a stamp that honored Sybil Ludington and proclaimed her a "Contributor to the Cause." Nationwide, 75,000 stamps were sold that day.[1]

# Acknowledgments

A RESEARCH PROJECT cannot go forward without the cooperation and combined knowledge of many people. It is with heartfelt appreciation that I recognize and thank the following people for their contributions to this project:

Wray Rominger of Purple Mountain Press for believing in Sybil and me enough to publish Sybil's story.

Andrew Campbell, technical clerk of the Mahopac Public Library, for his hard work on the bibliography and for his strong support and assistance throughout the project.

Pat Kaufman, Pat Miller, Hai-Ping Fu, Fran Harrison, and the staff at Mahopac Library.

The members of the weekly writing group at the Mahopac Public Library for their support, comments, and suggestions: Mia Stewart, Margaret Ryan, Marion Lyke, Lia Brennan, Rose Anzick, Alan Shils, and Jeanette van Dorp.

Richard A. Muscarella, Putnam County Historian, for his willingness to share his knowledge and contacts, and Sallie Sypher of his office.

Christine Mucciolo for her hard work and assistance.

Edward Lanyon Woodyard for his contribution of essential information on the Ogden-Connecticut connection.

Alan Kramer for his constant advice and support.

Everett J. Lee, historian for the Town of East Fishkill, N.Y., for his generous gift of four Sybil Ludington stamps and for sharing his personal file on Sybil.

Raymond Beecher, historian and volunteer librarian at the Greene County Historical Society's Vedder Memorial Research Center in Coxsakie, N.Y., for the excellent articles by Mabel Parker Smith. Also to Shirley McGrath and staff for their assistance.

Andrew Dancer III, Director of the Catskill Public Library, Catskill, N.Y., for his help with Sybil's Catskill years.

Wayne Wright at the New York State Historical Association in Cooperstown, N. Y., for his research assistance.

Tod Butler at the National Archives Research Center in Washington, D.C., for his assistance with the Richard and Edmund Ogden files.

William M. Grace of the Kansas State Historical Society for his aid with information on Edmund Augustus and Fort Riley.

Herbert F. Geller for his interview and the generous gift of his book, *A Fight for Liberty*, and Celeste Calvitto of the *Patent Trader* for her assistance in finding Mr. Geller's original articles.

Judy Allen, theater teacher/artist in residence for sharing a copy of her play, "Sibyl's Ride."

Sharyn Pratt of the Kent Historical Society for sharing information on the Ludingtons.

Alan Aimone, military reference specialist; Judith A. Sibley, archives curator; and Sheila Bibes, library technician, of the Special Collections and Archive Division, U.S.M.A. Library, West Point, N.Y.

Richard Marcello, village historian; Nancy Marcello, village librarian; and William Bauer, town historian, Unadilla, N.Y.

Staff members of The First Reformed Church of Latter Day Saints, Route 134, Yorktown Heights, N.Y., for their help in locating Edward Lanyon Woodyard.

Rev. Helen A. Havlik, pastor, the First Presbyterian Church of Unadilla for her information on early Unadilla.

Donald Ogden, Anna D. Ogden, and Fred Youmans of Walton, N.Y., for their material on Ogden genealogy.

Barbara Austin and Rod McKenzie of the Fairfield Historical Society for their help with early Ogden genealogy.

Sally Blakelock for her assistance with the records at St. Matthew's Church in Unadilla.

Warren and Verna Richards and Gertrude Genung Silbernell, long-time residents of Unadilla, for their discussions of old Unadilla.

Herb Carlson of the Unadilla Masons and the Staff at the Chancellor Robert R. Livingston Masonic Library of the Grand Lodge, 71 West 23rd Street, New York, N.Y., for their help with Henry Ogden's Masonic years.

Alfred and Lilian Eberhard and the members of the Carmel Historical Society.

Aileen Hayden from the Dutchess Historical Society for her help with Dutchess County research.

Steve Rovida, Derrek Barnes, Lorretta Barsanti, Marianne Mileno, Dan Callahan, and Lucille DeMeglio for their help with computer graphics.

Victoria K. Powell of the new Putnam County Archives Center for her help with proofreading and verifying sources.

Sandra L. Gray, seventh-grade social studies teacher in Newark Valley, N.Y., for her correspondence and information on textbooks that include mentions of Sybil.

Marion Brophy of Cooperstown for her research at the Otsego county clerk's office.

Pamela LeFever for her generous help with information on the Henry Ogden house and office.

Lincoln Diamant for his generous time and advice.

Nancy Ursprung of Catskill, N.Y., for sharing information on her home, the site of the former home and tavern of Sybil Ludington.

Barbara Rivette, daughter of Mabel Parker Smith, for sharing her mother's articles on the 1803 epidemic in Catskill.

Linda Miller of the BEPT Teachers' Center, Pelham, N.Y.

David Hayden for his hard work, patience, and editing skills.

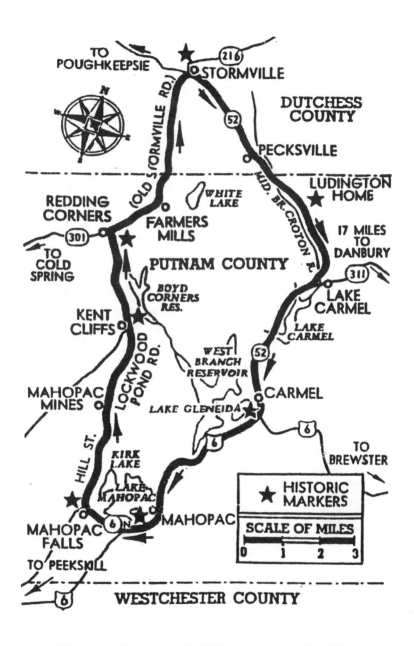

The probable route of Sybil Ludington's night ride
through what is now Putnam County, New York.

# Introduction

I CROSSED PATHS with Sybil Ludington one day in 1997 in the small hamlet of Mahopac Falls, 45 miles north of New York City. I was waiting at a stop sign when I noticed a road marker that said:

> Sybil Ludington rode horseback over this road the night of April 26, 1777, to call out Col. Ludington's regiment to repel the British at Danbury, Connecticut.

It wasn't the first time I had seen the sign, but it *was* the first time I actually read it.

As I drove away, it dawned on me that I had been oblivious to an important event of the American Revolution that had happened in my own neighborhood. I had no idea who Sybil Ludington was when I stopped, but that changed radically. My desire to learn more about her became a three-year obsession that took me to Washington, D.C., and through portions of New York State dozens of times. I began my research, however, right down the street from my house at the Mahopac Public Library.

"Of course we know of her," a young man with a ponytail and glasses said. "We have a whole vertical file on Sybil Ludington. Have you seen the statue of her down the road here on Lake Gleneida?"

Soon my arms were filled with magazine and newspaper clippings about a girl who made a perilous horseback ride similar to the one made by Paul Revere almost two years earlier, when he rode to rouse the countryside against the British.[2] But

The Presbyterian Church in Patterson, Putnam County, New York, where Sybil attended services with her parents and siblings and where she was married in 1784.

there the similarity ends. Revere was a renowned silversmith and a courier for the Massachusetts Assembly carrying messages to the Continental Congress, a man in his forties riding 12 miles of well-traveled country roads near Boston. Sybil was 16 years old, and her path led 40 miles through dense woods that harbored "Cowboys" and "Skinners." The Cowboys were pro-British marauders who roamed in and around Westchester County plundering farmhouses and stealing cattle they later sold to the British. The Skinners, named for General Courtland Skinner, had no regular organization. They were separate bands of mounted brigands who claimed attachment sometimes to the British and sometimes to the revolutionaries but were owned by neither. The Skinners did to the royalists what the Cowboys did to the revolutionaries. Together, they terrorized the countryside as they robbed and killed innocent victims, dragged men off to prisons, and molested women.

Henry Wadsworth Longfellow wrote a poem we all read in school about Paul Revere's exploits, but he did not mention that Revere was one of three men who undertook the mission

*Above:* Sybil's gravesite and road marker in Patterson, New York. *Below:* Sybil's gravestone behind the church where she is buried beside her parents. Edmond, Sybil's husband, is not buried in Patterson, and though we now know how he died, we do not know what happened to his remains.

and that he was arrested before he completed the ride. Sybil made her long journey alone, and she completed her mission. She received little attention in her time, yet her story was preserved within her family and passed down through generations. Finally in 1907, 130 years after the event, details of her ride emerged as part of the family's memoirs.

Over the next 30 years, the DAR fought to get recognition for Sybil's achievement. The result was the road marker I had seen and others that were placed along her route. Other honors followed: a bronze equestrian statue of her created by the world-famous sculptor, Anna Hyatt Huntington, in 1961; an eight-cent United States postage stamp dedicated in her honor in 1975; an opera written by Susan Schefflein and Ludmila Ulehla; countless poems and papers by school children; and at least two long narrative poems.

In much of the published material, however, errors occurred, mistakes that need to be rectified. I had no intention of writing a book about Sybil Ludington when I first sought to discover who she was, but I believe now that a biography about her is imperative to correct the misconceptions I have found. Published information about Sybil's life is sparse, untrue, or difficult to locate. Dates often contradict each other. Simple facts, such as her husband's first name and occupation, where and how he died, where she lived after the ride, and even the number of children she had have been incorrect for years and repeated without being checked.

Letters, public records, articles, books, and even a letter signed by Sybil herself, have helped me piece together my view of the life of Sybil Ludington.

I feel that Sybil herself has been my inspiration for this book. Every attempt was made to present her accurately with as much information as possible. This biography, developed with the help of many people, is in essence my fight for Sybil's right to be known for who she was in the world in which she lived.

# Before Sybil's Ride

SYBIL LUDINGTON was the eldest of the 12 children of Abigail and Henry Ludington. Henry was born in Branford, Connecticut, on May 25, 1739, the son of William and Mary (Knowles) Ludington.[3] Abigail, his first cousin, was born in Rumbout Patent in Southern Dutchess County on May 8, 1745. She was the daughter of Elisha, the tenth child of the Colonel's uncle.[4]

Henry met Abigail when he was on his way to Quebec with Connecticut troops during the French and Indian War. A somewhat romantic account of their meeting was included in Willis Fletcher Johnson's memoir of Colonel Ludington in 1907: "As the Connecticut troops on their way to that war marched across Dutchess County, New York, through Dover [Plains] and Amenia, it is to be presumed that Henry Ludington on that momentous journey called at his uncle's home, and saw his cousin, afterward to be his wife, who. . .was at that time consequently a child of about ten years. . .but we may easily imagine the boy soldier's carrying with him into the northern wilderness an affectionate memory of his little cousin, perhaps the last of his kin to bid him good-by, and also her cherishing a romantic regard for the lad whom she had seen march away with his comrades."[5]

After the Canadian campaign, on May 1, 1760, Henry and Abigail were married. The following April, Sybil was born, and soon after the young family moved to Dutchess County, New York, and settled on 229 acres of undeveloped land in the Philipse Patent. Later the Patent became the Fredericksburgh

Precinct of Dutchess County. In 1812, it became part of the
Town of Kent in Putnam County.

When the Ludingtons arrived, they were surrounded by
dense wilderness. The land was fertile and cheap, pasture for
the stock abundant, and the water good; overall, the place was
healthy, pleasant, and free from many of the problems of other
new settlements. With persistence, determination, and the cooperation of their growing family, Henry and Abigail struggled
to make the new land their home. While young Abigail rose to
her duties as mother and wife, Henry occupied a position of
influence, respect, and authority.

Little is known of Abigail's life other than the fact that she
bore 11 more children after Sybil. Her courage was crucial to
the development of their wilderness life during one of colonial
America's most difficult times. Her everyday struggles did not
defeat her—she raised 12 children and stood by Henry as he
played his role as soldier and citizen. She lived to be 80 years

---

### Ludington Family Tree

Children of William and Ellen Ludington

| Thomas | John | Mary | Henry | Hannah | William II | Matthew |
|--------|------|------|-------|--------|-----------|---------|

m. Martha Rose
Henry ———————————————— Daniel
Eleanor                           William
William              Submit       Sarah
                     Mary         Dinah
m. Mary Whitehead    Henry        Lydia
Mercy                Lydia        Nathaniel
Mary                 Samuel       Moses
Hannah               Rebecca      Aaron
John                 Anne         Elisha (died an infant)
Eliphalet            Stephen      Elisha ———————— Comfort
Elizabeth                         Sarah           Asa
Dorothy                           Thomas          Lydia
Dorcas                                            Elisha
                                                  Abigail
                    married ——————————————————————

**Sybil**   Rebecca   Mary   Archibald   Henry    Derick
Tertullus   Abigail   Anna   Frederick   Sophia   Lewis

old in a time when many people died before they were 50. Abigail died on August 3, 1825.

Henry was a prominent figure and a subject of interest to historians. "The Colonel," as he was known for most of his life, appears to us in numerous accounts of the times. Above medium height, with blue eyes, he was a husky man with military bearing. As a businessman, he was successful, irreproachable, and determined. In spite of the demands of his mill, his farm, and his family, he was diligent in fulfilling his civic and military duties. He was a member of the New York Assembly from 1777 to 1781, and again in 1786. He was a justice of the peace, town supervisor, and overseer of the poor. He also served as sub-sheriff and church trustee for many years, and as a member of the Committee of Safety, which was considered the law in many places.

Henry Ludington even became involved with spies. "John Jay was the acting Judge for this section of Dutchess. Jay and Ludington employed several secret agents to ferret out Tory activities and many prisoners were taken to Judge Jay. Enoch Crosby, who was made famous by James Fenimore Cooper as Harvey Birch in *The Spy*, spent much time at the Ludington home and had a code of secret signals known to Sybil and her sister Rebecca, who were always on guard during their father's absence.[6]

In all, Henry served his community and country for more than 60 years. His military career began when he was 17 years old, in 1756, when he enlisted in the 2nd Regiment of Connecticut—troops in the service of the king. He took part in the French and Indian War from 1756 to 1769 and participated in the Battle of Lake George in 1755, where he witnessed the horrors of war. His uncle and a cousin were mortally wounded as they fought by his side. Still, he reenlisted and in 1759 was detailed to escort a company of invalid soldiers from Canada to Boston. The march was made in the dead of winter, and on many nights, with only a blanket for protection, he was forced to dig himself into snowdrifts to avoid freezing. When his rations finally ran out, he ate the bark and twigs of birch trees and berries that he scavenged from the frozen countryside. Nonetheless, he survived to complete his mission.[7]

Soon after Henry arrived in Dutchess County in 1761, he became sub-sheriff and swore an oath to remain faithful to the king, "to defend Him against all traitorous conspiracies and attempts against his person, crown, and dignity to the utmost of his power, and particularly to uphold the succession of the crown against the claims of the pretended Prince of Wales, who had styled himself King of England under the name of James the Third."[8]

William Tryon, the captain-general and governor of the Province of New York, appointed Henry as Captain of the Fifth Company of the Second Battalion of the Fredericksburgh Regiment of Militia in Dutchess County. On February 13, 1773, Henry accepted a commission as captain in Colonel Beverly Robinson's Dutchess County regiment. Soon after, his loyalty to the king dwindled and he resigned his commission in favor of the revolutionary cause.

It was a period in American history when enemies could live next door or hide waiting and armed behind trees or near an outhouse. Real battles with loss of life occurred in taverns and in skirmishes in back yards between revolutionaries and their royalist neighbors and former friends. Family arguments began in one-room schoolhouses and in April planting fields, where men tended the land, ready in an instant to respond to the call for battle in defense of their families.

Henry's military experience influenced the Patriot's Provincial Congress of the Colony of New York to appoint him to the rank of colonel in the summer of 1776. A new provincial congress, calling itself the Convention of the Representatives of the State of New York, also commissioned Henry as a colonel. His regiment, the Seventh of the Dutchess County militia, was thereafter referred to as Colonel Ludington's regiment.

Colonel Ludington's area of command in Dutchess County was along the most direct route the British might take to and from Connecticut and the coast on Long Island Sound. He was forced to bring his regiment into "active and constant service in the counties of Dutchess and Westchester, either to assist the regular troops, or to quell the turbulent Tory spirit of that section, or to repress the vicious and exasperating conduct of the 'Cowboys and Skinners. . . .' "[9]

One record described the Colonel's section as "deplorable." "Small parties of volunteers on one side, and parties of Royalists and Tories on the other, constantly harassed the inhabitants and plundered without mercy friend and foe alike. To guard against surprise required the utmost vigilance. Within this territory resided many friends of the American cause, whose situation exposed them to continual ravages by Tories, horse thieves, and cowboys, who robbed them indiscriminately and mercilessly, while the personal abuse and punishment were almost incredible."[10]

Colonel Ludington and his regiment often prevented marauders from obtaining supplies for the British forces. Much of General Howe's cattle and grain came from Cowboys and thieves. The Colonel's success enraged Howe who put a price on Colonel Ludington's head of 300 English guineas, "dead or alive!"[11]

Henry was also deeply involved in his family life and in the workings of his farm and his gristmill and sawmill. Erected in 1776, the gristmill was the first in the region. It enjoyed a fine reputation for quality milling and had the distinction of being built almost solely by women because most of the men were away in military service.[12]

Henry and Abigail raised 12 children in the Ludington house. Their births were recorded in the Colonel's family

# THE LUDINGTON HOME

OVER THE YEARS, the Ludington home became famous far and wide for showing good cheer to travelers. Guests received the warmest hospitality. The Ludingtons entertained General Washington, General Rochambeau, William Ellery of Massachusetts, a signer of the Declaration of Independence, among many others. The Colonel is said to have lived his later years there entertaining and sitting with friends, such as John Jay, to smoke his pipe and exchange stories about the days of the Revolution.*

The Ludington house has been described as

built prior to the revolution and in style similar to almost every house of the period, two stories in the front and one in the rear. Huge doors divided in the middle with ponderous latches gave entrance. A piazza. . .large and spacious rooms, their ceilings low and the floors nicely sanded ornamented the front. Wide halls divided the rooms; a massive stairway led up to the commodious chambers. Immense chimneys rose within the structures, each with wide fireplaces and large ovens.**

Another source states the house was

several times enlarged. The main building was two stories in height, with an attic above. Through the center ran a broad hall, with a stairway broken with a landing and turn. At one side was a parlor and at the other a sitting or living room, and back of each of these was a bedroom. The parlor was wainscoted and ceiled with planks of the fragrant and beautiful red cedar. Beyond the sitting room, at the side of this main building, was the "weaving" room, an apartment unknown to our domestic economy, but essential in colonial days. It was a large room fitted with a handloom, and a number of spinning wheels, reels, swifts, and the other paraphernalia for the manufacture of homespun fabrics of different kinds. This room also contained a huge stone fireplace. Beyond it, at the extreme east of the house, was the kitchen, with its great fireplace and brick or stone oven. The house fronted toward the south, and commanded a fine outlook over one of the picturesque landscapes for which that region is famed.***

In 1838, 76 years after the Ludingtons moved to Dutchess County and one year before Sybil died, the Ludington house was torn down.

The Ludington Mill consisted of a post-and-girt frame, fastened with wooden pegs and hand-wrought square nails. The building was 24 by 36 feet and was two-and-one-half stories high. It was built in 1776 and destroyed by a fire in 1972, just months before it was to be restored by the Putnam County Historical Society.

*Dutchess County Historical Society Year Book, Vol. 25, 1940: 81.
**Patrick, 273.
***Johnson, 39-40.

register and inscribed on the flyleaf of one of the ledgers he used in his many capacities as a public servant:[13]

Sibyl, April 5, 1761.
Rebecca, January 24, 1763.
Mary, July 31, 1765.
Archibald, July 5, 1767.
Henry, March 28, 1769.
Derick, February 17, 1771.
Tertullus, Monday Night, April 19, 1773.
Abigail, Monday Morning, February 26, 1776.
Anna, at sunset, March 14, 1778.
Frederick, June 10, 1782.
Sophia, May 16, 1784.
Lewis, June 25, 1786.

On the surface, Sybil's life was free from many of the hardships of the time. Her parents were far from poor, and her father had great influence in the county. However, she bore many burdens on her young shoulders. The oldest of 12 children, she was expected to take a prominent role in raising her siblings. In addition, she had to face the reality that her father might leave home some morning and never return or that a shot could ring out at any time and take him as he sat at the family table. Sybil's world of "simple country-girl prosperity" was actually a complex maze of uncertainty, fear, and bravery. Given the turmoil of the times, Sybil was compelled to take a leading role in protecting her father, who was a wanted man. An incident recounted by Lewis S. Patrick illustrates the extent of her commitment toward this end.

One night Ichobod Prosser, a notorious Tory, came with hopes of getting the large reward posted on the Colonel's head. Prosser's men surrounded the house and prepared to attack, but Sybil and her sister Rebecca outsmarted them:

These fearless girls, with guns in hand were acting as sentinels, pacing the piazza to and fro in true military style and grit to guard their father against surprise and to give him warning of any approaching danger. They discovered Prosser and his men and gave the alarm. In a flash, candles were lighted in every room of the house and the few occupants marched and counter-marched before the windows and from this simple and clever ruse, Prosser was led to believe that the house was strongly guarded and did not dare to make an attack. He kept his men concealed behind the trees and fences until daybreak, when with yells they resumed their march and hastened southwards toward New York City, ignorant of how they had been foiled by clever girls. The Colonel's most vigilant and watchful companion was his sentinel daughter, Sibbell. Her constant care and thoughtfulness, combined with fortuitous circumstances, prevented the fruition of many an intrigue against his life and capture.[14]

Into this tense situation, a chain of events began that challenged Sybil's courage to the utmost—the British march on Danbury, Connecticut, and the subsequent burning of that city.

The commissioners of the Continental Army had been using Danbury as a depot for military stores, and British General William Tryon was assigned to prevent their use by enemies of the king. On April 24, 1777, 20 transports and six war vessels left New York Harbor for Compo Beach in Connecticut. Troops reached Compo the next day and debarked, ready to begin the long march to Danbury. Tryon's men proceeded as if on parade. One soldier was described in detail:

Upon his head a metallic cap, sword-proof, surmounted by a cone, from which a long, chestnut-colored plume fell to his shoulders. Upon the front of the cap was a death's head, under which was inscribed the words: "Or Glory." A red coat faced with white, an epaulette on each shoulder, buckskin breeches of a bright yellow, black knee boots, and spurs completing the costume. A long sword swung at his side, and a carbine was carried, muzzle down, in a socket at his stirrup.

These were models of discipline and military splendor, and
mounted on handsome chargers, sixteen hands high."[15]

Another detachment, the 64th Foot—a grenadier regiment,
wore "high grenadier caps and red coats faced with black." This
"parade" of the king's forces marched steadily through Connecticut toward an unsuspecting Danbury.

Word spread ahead of the British, and Connecticut revolutionaries mustered to resist as best they could along the route
of the march. Generals David Wooster and Benedict Arnold,
receiving intelligence at New Haven, gathered a small escort
and pushed westward, picking up various militia companies as
they advanced. Meanwhile, General Gold Selleck Silliman with
500 militiamen was already on the trail of Tryon. Colonel
Henry Ludington came in from New York with 400 reinforce-
ments.

One Connecticut regiment, known as "The Gallant Seventeen," hid in the shadows of the moonlit night waiting to
ambush the advancing column. They struck out of the dark-
ness, killing a number of soldiers, with only one American
slightly wounded, but they did not stop the march. The British
loaded their dead and wounded in an oxcart, sent them back to
the ships, and continued on. After passing what is now called
Aspetuck, the royalist troops stopped in the parish of Weston,
where they probably rested.

Rumors spread like wildfire among the threatened citizens.
One story that reached Redding held that General Tryon was
out to kill young boys because they would grow into soldiers.
"The women of Redding had heard of this propensity and at
his approach gathered all the boys of thirteen and under. . .and
conveyed them to a secluded place near[by] where they were
left under the charge of one Gershom Barlow. Here they
remained until the invader had regained his ships, provisions
being cooked and sent to them daily."[16]

One Redding mother, Rebecca Sanford Barlow, earned a
place in history because she stayed with her sick children to face

the enemy while most of her neighbors fled in fear. "The terrified inhabitants resolved on instant flight. Each family gathered together such of their effects as they could take with them and quickly quit the village, traveling the whole night to reach a place of refuge. Mrs. Barlow had two sick children and could not carry them away. To leave them was out of the question, so she and her family remained alone to face the enemy, deserted by all her neighbors."[17] Some hid in barns and forests, others escaped the area with all the goods they could gather in carts and wagons. Parents had to face the horrifying decision whether to accompany their families to safety or stay and do what they could to secure their homes against the enemy.

In a place called Couch's Rock in Weston, Connecticut, a small regiment of revolutionaries under Captain Zalmon Read met with British troops in full force and was immediately taken captive with no fatalities, sending a clear message that this was an enemy to be reckoned with. From there, the British troops moved across the Weston border into Redding and proceeded through the town causing no destruction or casualties. At Redding's Ridge, they stopped for breakfast and relaxed in the comfort of royalist hospitality. At the time, Redding was known as "Tory country." Although no buildings were destroyed, several prisoners were taken.

Before reaching Danbury, the 2,000-man British force had to pass through Bethel, Connecticut. Rain fell heavily throughout the night causing difficult conditions for soldiers on both sides. A man named Luther Holcomb put the British army on edge by marching to the top of a hill pretending to be followed by a number of troops. "Halt the whole universe! Break off by kingdoms and prepare to attack!" he shouted. The British believed him enough to prepare for battle, but when it was realized that there would be no attack, they marched quietly out of Bethel in the rain without incident. As they left, American troops slipped in quietly behind them at 11:30 P.M. under

the direction of Generals Benedict Arnold, David Wooster, and
Gold Selleck Silliman. Together they ordered 600 men to
prepare to fight the British in the pouring rain with muskets
that could barely shoot in dry weather. They waited in Bethel
for the return of the British, hoping for a surprise attack, but
Tryon brought his troops back through Ridgefield after his
night in Danbury.

On the following afternoon, the enemy reached Danbury
in sunshine between two and three o'clock, but another storm
was on its way bringing the additional heavy rains that Sybil
would be forced to ride through that night. As the afternoon
continued, a few incidents occurred. British soldiers chased one
horseman through the streets. He escaped when he unrolled a
bolt of cloth he was carrying and frightened a pursuer's horse.
A second incident involved four young men who shot into a
column of soldiers from the house of Captain Ezra Starr, which
was raided immediately after the shots rang out. The house was
burned along with the bodies of the men who had been accused
of the shooting.

As the day proceeded, British soldiers continued to take
control of Danbury. "As the British troops reached a point near
the present location of the court-house their artillery was
discharged and the heavy balls, six and twelve-pounders, flew
screaming up the street, carrying terror to the hearts of the
women and children, and dismay to the heads of the homes thus
endangered."[18]

John Porter came into the village to see what was happen-
ing. Porter was "a man of powerful build, with muscles like
steel, and a movement that was a very good substitute for
lightning." When he was to told to halt, he stood tall against
them, and asked, "What for?" He advanced on them, and they
said, "You are our prisoner." He continued his move on them.
"Guess not," he said. They were close upon him, but there was
a gully behind them. In a flash he had the foremost trooper in
his grasp. In the next instant, he hurled him against the other

two, and the three of them tumbled into the gully in a demor-
alized heap. The rest of the squad, seeing the disaster, immediately surrounded and subdued Porter. Porter and a man named
Barnum are believed to be the only prisoners the enemy carried
away from Danbury. They were thrown into a New York
prison called Sugar House Prison. Porter was released eventually, but Barnum later died there of starvation.[19]

British troops remained in Danbury all day destroying
patriot military stores. Those goods found in a Church of
England and goods found in the homes of royalists were taken
into the street to be burned and their buildings spared, but
houses owned by revolutionaries used as storehouses for grain
and meat were burned to the ground. "It is said that the fat from
the burning meat ran ankle-deep in the street. No less free ran
the rum and wine, although not in the same direction!"

As night began, drunken brawls and loud laughter became
more frequent. "The drunken men went up and down Main
Street in squads, singing army songs, shouting coarse speeches,
hugging each other, swearing, yelling, and otherwise conduct-
ing themselves as becomes an invader when he is very, very
drunk."[20]

During some of the day and most of the night, Connecticut
farmers sneaked back into the enemy camp to kill an occasional
soldier. All around them revolutionary troops were being
mustered until finally, General Tryon gave an order to move
out.

By midnight, three Danbury buildings had been burned and
many of the drunken revelers were sleeping soundly. By about
one o'clock Sunday morning, Tryon ordered the gathering of
soldiers and the work of real destruction began. More buildings
were burned. Those owned by Tories were marked with a
cross, which protected them; houses without crosses were
torched.

## LEWIS S. PATRICK

LEWIS S. PATRICK is acknowledged on page 219 of the Ludington memoirs as a "great-grandson of Colonel Henry Ludington, through his son Frederick and the latter's daughter Caroline." Johnson credits Patrick as follows: "To his painstaking and untiring labors must be credited the collection of a large share of the data used upon which this memoir of his ancestor is founded."* Note that the Johnson spelling of "Lewis" does not agree with the spelling of "Louis" in an article in the *Connecticut Magazine*, but it is likely they are one and the same person. Much of the information in the 1907 article is nearly identical to information in the memoirs. "Louis" S. Patrick was a respected historian. In his *Connecticut Magazine* article he was referred to as one "who has made an extended study of this phase of the American Revolution."

*Johnson, 219

In the meantime, as the flames filled a rainy night sky, dispatchers rode frantically in all directions, and American troops rallied to a belated defense of Danbury.

Before long, a rider roused the Ludington household, and Sybil was galloping into the night on her way to muster the Colonel's regiment. W. F. Johnson told the story of her ride in 1907. It is presumed that he based his information on the records of Lewis S. Patrick, the Colonel's great-grandson.[21]

According to Johnson:

At eight or nine o'clock that evening a jaded horseman reached Colonel Ludington's home with the news. We may imagine the fire that flashed through the veteran's veins at the report of the dastardly act of his former chief. [General Tryon, the last of the British governors of New York, had appointed Colonel Ludington a captain in a colonial regiment before the Colonel became a revolutionary.] But what to do? His regiment was disbanded; its members scattered at their homes, many at considerable distances. [It was April, planting season, and the farmers needed to tend their fields and were granted leaves to get their farm work done.] He must stay there to muster all who came in. The messenger from Danbury could ride no more, and there was no neighbor within call. In this emergency he turned to his daughter Sybil, who, a few days before, had passed her sixteenth birthday, and bade her to take a horse, ride for the men, and tell them to be at his house by daybreak. One who even rides now from Carmel to Cold Spring will find rugged and dangerous roads, with lonely stretches. Imagination only can picture what it was a quarter and a century ago [now over two centuries ago] on a dark night, with reckless bands of "Cowboys" and "Skinners" abroad in the land. But the child performed her task, clinging to a man's saddle, and guiding her steed with only a hempen halter, as she rode through the night, bearing the news of the sack of Danbury. There is no extravagance in comparing her ride with that of Paul Revere and its midnight message. Nor was her errand less efficient than his was. By daybreak, thanks to her daring, nearly the whole regiment was mustered before her father's house at Fredricksburgh, and an hour or two later was on the march for vengeance on the raiders.[22]

In this dramatic rendition of Sybil's ride, Johnson is not correct when he refers to Sybil as a "child." Sybil's world wasn't the world we live in today. Sybil's mother, Abigail, for example, was only fifteen when she married Henry. Sybil was a very capable young woman at sixteen and was engaged in the revolutionary cause beyond just helping to protect her father or doing domestic chores. The story of her conspiring with Enoch Crosby, a notorious spy, attests to this fact. Sybil also knew the roads and where the men lived, perhaps as a result of riding with her father along the narrow, dirt roads of Mahopac and Carmel. They undoubtedly laid out the best route to be used to muster the regiment in times of emergency. It is doubtful that she had to rouse each of the 400 men individually. Key people in each village heard her banging on their shutters, and in turn, alerted the local contingent while she rode on to complete her mission. In the morning, Colonel Ludington's regiment was gathered in his yard, preparing to face the enemy.

During the night, Tryon was forced to make several decisions. Earlier hopes to take captured supplies to New York City for British use were abandoned. Additional supplies would slow him down and make it impossible to fight those on their way to engage him. He chose instead to burn as much of the stores as possible to prevent their use by the revolutionaries. He was also forced to abandon any plans of invading Dutchess and Westchester Counties. The next morning, Sunday, April 27, it was clear to General Tyron that he would have to make it back to Compo by way of Ridgefield and get his men aboard the ships as quickly as possible to avoid the troops at Bethel.[23] General Alexander McDougall was marching in from Peekskill, and Colonel Ludington was on his way from Dutchess County. By this time, however, the troops from Bethel had crossed over into Ridgefield. McDougall had 1,200 men to support the 600 to 800 from Bethel. Behind them were the troops from Dutchess County consisting of another 400 men. Johnson described them this way:

> They were a motley company, some without arms, some half dressed, but all filled with a certain berserk rage. That night they reached Redding and joined Arnold, Wooster, and Silliman. The next morning they encountered the British at Ridgefield. They were short of ammunition and were outnumbered by the British three to one. But they practiced the same tactics that Paul Revere's levies at Lexington and Concord found so effective. Their scattering sharpshooter fire from behind trees and fences and stone walls, harassed the British sorely, and made their retreat to their ships at Compo resemble a rout. Nor were instances of individual heroism in conflict lacking. Arnold had his horse shot from under him as, almost alone, he furiously charged the enemy, and the

gallant Wooster received a wound from which he died a few days later. There were far greater operations in the war than this, but there was scarcely one more expeditious, intrepid and successful. Writing of it to Gouverneur Morris, Alexander Hamilton said, "I congratulate you on the Danbury expedition. The stores destroyed there have been purchased at a high price to the enemy. The spirit of the people on the occasion does them great honor—is a pleasing proof that they have lost nothing of that primitive zeal with which they began the contest, and will be a galling discouragement to the enemy from repeating attempts of the kind. The people of New York considered the affair in the light of a defeat to the troops."[24]

Tryon reached Ridgefield more slowly than he had expected, and after burning a mill belonging to Isaac Keeler, stopped his troops for lunch and rest just outside North Salem. At that point, General Wooster attacked Tryon but was counterattacked. Wooster retreated but returned. On his return and attack of the rear guard, he was fatally wounded.

Captain Stephen Rowe Bradley assumed command of Wooster's troops. His company went on to join General Arnold, who was still highly respected; it would be three years until his infamous betrayal. During the battle, a cannonball was fired into the nearby Keeler Tavern.

Not far from the tavern is a memorial to the soldiers from Ridgefield who fought in the battle of 1777. It commemorates: "eight Patriots, who were laid in these grounds, companioned by sixteen British soldiers living, their enemies; dying their guests."

Tryon burned several homes in Ridgefield and went on to burn more houses and destroy more supplies in Wilton before making his way to the Saugatuck River and Compo Beach. General Tryon's officers, however, reported 50 to 60 enlisted men and five officers killed or wounded in the two-hour battle at Ridgefield alone.

# GENERAL DAVID WOOSTER

A SMALL PLAQUE hangs adjacent to present-day Route 116 in Ridgefield to mark the spot where Wooster was shot. A small-engraved stone and sign were placed on what is now a busy thoroughfare.

An excerpt from his obituary published in "Historical Collections of Connecticut" reads:

> The British had six pieces of artillery, three in the front and three guarding the rear. The screaming of the grape-shot and the whistling of the balls frightened the militiamen and they hesitated in charging. Wooster endeavored to rally them, and turning in his saddle shouted, "Come on, my boys, never mind such random shots!" While leading his men and before he had time to turn his face toward the enemy. . .he was struck by the fatal musket ball. He fell from his horse and his sash was stripped from him and used to bear him from the field of battle. . . . The bullet, which is said to have been fired by a Tory, entered his back obliquely, just as he turned to wave on his men. . . . On Friday, May 2d, he died. On Sunday the funeral was held. It was a quiet affair, although the body was that of a major-general and of a soldier who for courage and patriotism had no superior.*

*Case, 43-44

*Above:* Keeler's Tavern. On April 27, 1777, during the battle of Ridgefield, British troops advanced down Main Street and fired on the tavern because revolutionaries were reported to be making musket balls in the cellar. Today the tavern is a museum open to the public. A small cannonball fired that day is still embedded behind an old shingle on the side of the main house. Viewing the ball is part of a tour. *Below:* Memorial for the Battle of Ridgefield where eight revolutionaries and 16 British soldiers were killed.

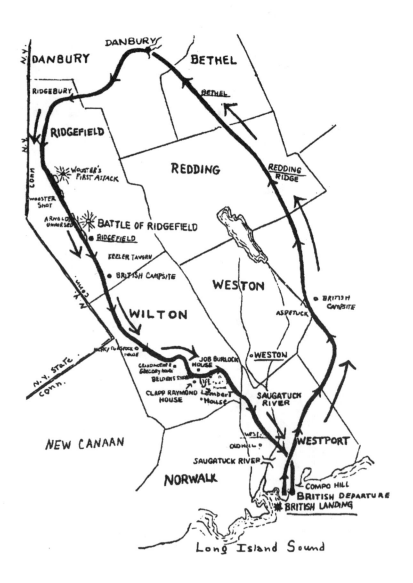

British General William Tryon's raid, April 26-28, 1777.

# THE LOSS OF PATRIOT SUPPLIES

RECORDS obtained from General Howe's official report stated that "in the destruction of the stores at Danbury, the village was unavoidably burnt." He listed the materials lost: "a quantity of ordnance stores, with iron, etc.; 4000 barrels of beef and pork; 100 large tierces of biscuits; 89 barrels of rice; 120 puncheons of rum; several large stores of wheat, oats and Indian corn, in bulk, the quantity hereof could not be ascertained; 30 pipes of wine; 100 hogsheads of sugar; 50 dittos of molasses; 20 casks of coffee; 15 large casks filled with medicines of all kinds; 10 barrels of saltpeter; 1020 tents and marquees; a number of iron boilers; a large quantity of hospital bedding; engineer's, pioneer's and carpenter's tools; a printing press complete; tar, tallow, etc.; 5000 pairs of shoes and stockings."[*]

A committee appointed by the Connecticut General Assembly in May 1777 recorded the losses of 19 dwelling houses, the meetinghouse of the New Danbury Society, and 22 stores and barns, with all of their houses consumed. Howe reported British casualties as "One drummer and fife, and 23 rank and file killed; 3 field officers, 6 captains, 3 subalterns, 9 sergeants, 92 rank and file wounded; 1 drummer and fifer and 27 rank and file missing. Royal artillery: 2 additional killed, 3 matrosses and 1 wheeler wounded, and 1 matross missing."

"Return of the rebels killed and wounded" were listed: "Killed: General Wooster; Colonel Gould; Colonel Lamb, of the artillery; Colonel Henman; Dr. Atwater, a man of considerable influence; Captain Cooe; Lieutenant Thompson; 100 privates; Wounded: Colonel Whiting; Captain Benjamin; Lieutenant Cooe; 250 privates. Taken: fifty privates, including several committeemen."

[*]James R. Case, *Tryon's Raid: Published on the Occasion of the One Hundred and Fiftieth Anniversary* (Danbury, 1927), 28.

# Sybil

THE ACCOUNT of Sybil's heroic journey remained family legend until 1907 when Louis S. Patrick wrote his article in the *Connecticut Magazine* revealing the details of the historic ride. In that same year, W. F. Johnson authored a book commissioned and published by two of Henry Ludington's grandchildren, Lavinia Elizabeth and Charles Henry Ludington. The memoirs, originally published for the family, aroused considerable public interest and local pride in Sybil's achievement. In 1912, Reverend George Noble of Carmel composed a lengthy poem inspired by the information provided by Patrick and Johnson. The poem kept Sybil in the public light but did not gain the fame of Longfellow's poem about Paul Revere.

In 1925, Sybil again reached public attention when a program promoting observances for the sesquicentennial of the American War for Independence began. The goal of The American Scenic and Historic Preservation Society was to mark historical places and objects along or near highways. The society received assistance in Putnam County from the Enoch Crosby Chapter, Daughters of the American Revolution. After hearing Sybil's story from George Turner, a Ludington relative, it was suggested that her ride be marked with New York State Education Department signs. The idea was approved, and dozens of markers were proposed. By 1935, the site of Sybil's home, where she began her ride, and her route were clearly marked for public interest.[25]

Berton Braley, a nationally recognized poet, published another poem about Sybil in the *New York Herald Tribune*'s "This

Week's Magazine," April 14, 1940. Braley's poem sparked new attention, and Sybil's heroic deed finally caught the public's imagination.

In 1959, internationally renowned sculptor Anna Hyatt Huntington created a bronze equestrian statue of Sybil. It was dedicated on June 3, 1961, in Carmel, New York, Putnam County. A three-foot replica of the statue stands in the plaza of the Danbury Public Library.

Congressman Robert R. Barry of New York presented an 18-inch reproduction of the statue on the grounds of the National Women's Party headquarters on May 18, 1963. He addressed the House of Representatives two days later, where he referred to the ceremony: "I place in the Records my remarks made at the unveiling. I would also like to add the text of a ballad entitled, 'The Ride of Sybil Ludington,' written by Mrs. Marjorie Barstowe Greenbie, and arranged and movingly sung at the ceremony by Mr. and Mrs. Charles Perdue, of Fairfax, Virginia.[26]

Barry also shared a resolution made and passed unanimously by the National Women's Party that he then entered in the *Congressional Record* (Vol. 109, No. 75, page A3168):

The best tribute we can bring to Sibyl Ludington is to go forward ourselves in the present-day campaign for the complete freedom of American women—with the same courage, the same determination, the same intensity of conviction that the heroic young Sibyl Ludington displayed in her famous ride for the freedom of the American colonists from the control of the Government and laws of England.

*Be it resolved, therefore,* That we send from this gathering a group or spokesman to urge the Senate Committee on Constitutional Amendments, to give its powerful aid, with all possible energy, and all possible speed to bringing final victory, through the passage of the equal rights amendment, the struggle of more than 300 years by American women for complete release from the bondage of the ancient Common Law of England, which largely controls the lives of American women today, even as in still greater degree it controlled the lives of American women in the days of Sybil Ludington 186 years ago.

Another feather in the young hero's cap came on Tuesday, March 26, 1975, when she rode her way onto a U.S. postage stamp. Ceremonies marking the issuance of the 35th U.S. stamp to honor a woman drew hundreds of people to Carmel, New York.

With interest in Sybil Ludington aroused, many local newspapers and magazines began writing articles about her historic ride. Two women, Ludmila Ulehla of Long Island and Susan Schefflein of Putnam Valley, created "Sybil of the American Revolution," an opera performed at the Abigail Adams Smith Museum in New York City on April 1, 1993. "Sibyl's Ride: A Biographical Play about Sibyl Ludington" written by Judy Allen is performed by children in schools and parks throughout Putnam County. Social studies teachers introduce Sybil to their fourth-grade classes as part of their regular curriculum.

Sybil's rise in popularity created an increasing desire to know more about the teenage hero. However, information about her personal life has been difficult to uncover. To complicate matters, nothing previously published about Sybil was without error, which makes research on Sybil very exciting but sometimes very confusing. Information about her marriage and children, where she lived and how long, and even her husband's first name was unclear. A popular biographical piece, "Girl Who Outrode Paul Revere," appeared in *Coronet*, November 1949, but it was woefully incorrect. Its misinformation has been quoted time and again in articles about Sybil:

> And what became of Sybil Ludington? At 23, she married her childhood sweetheart, Edmond Ogden, and through the years gave him four sons and two daughters. Two of her boys became officers in the Army of the United States. One of them—E. A. Ogden—after serving with distinction through

the Blackhawk, Seminole, and Mexican Wars, lived to found Fort Riley, Kansas, where a monument has been erected to him.

Congressman Barry repeated this paragraph word for word in the *Congressional Record*. Unfortunately, Edmond was not Sybil's childhood sweetheart. She did not have six children, and her son did not "serve with distinction" in any war. In the March/April 1989 issue of *New York Alive*, an article entitled "The Midnight Ride of Sibyl Ludington" by Robert W. Pelton quoted the 1949 *Coronet* article word for word. Historical novels and articles today perpetuate the erroneous information or avoid biographical details altogether.

The source of some misinformation was an error that appeared first in Pelletreau's *History of Putnam County, New York*, published in 1886. It included biographical information about the Ludington children, but stated that Sybil married a man named *Henry* Ogden. The list below is as it appeared:

Sybil, born April 5, 1761, died 1839, married Henry Ogden;
Rebecca, born January 24, 1763, married Henry Pratt, May 7th, 1794;
Mary, born July 31st, 1765, married David Travis, September 12th, 1785;
Archibald, born July 5th, 1767;
Henry, 2d, born March 28th, 1769; went to Catskill (his sons, Lewis and Joseph, were the builders of three of the "monitors");
Derick, born February 17th, 1771, died unmarried, December, 1840;
Tertullus, born April 19th, 1773;
Abigail, born February 26th, 1776;
Anna, born March 14th, 1778, married Joseph Colwell;
Frederick, born June 10th, 1782, died July 23d, 1852;
Sophia, born May 16th, 1784, married Mr. Ferris;
Lewis, born June 25th, 1786, died September 3d, 1857[27]

While this information on the Ludington children was of genealogical interest, it had devastating effects for Sybil researchers. Sybil Ludington never married a *Henry* Ogden; she married *Edmond* Ogden and had a *son* named Henry.

Interestingly, Pelletreau added a footnote stating: "A grandson of Sybil, Major Edmund A. Ogden of the United States Army, died at Fort Riley, Kansas Territory, in 1855, where the soldiers under him built a monument to his memory." This information is correct, but many historians and journalists apparently ignored the footnote, because they listed Major Edmund A. Ogden as Sybil's *son.*

In 1897, J. B. Beers published *A Commemorative Biographical Record of the Counties of Putnam and Dutchess New York* that again listed Sybil's husband as *Henry* Ogden.[28] Beers, however, omitted Pelletreau's footnote about Sybil's grandson with the result that later researchers, relying on Beers, gave Major E. A. Ogden as Sybil's *son* and not as her grandson—an error that has been repeated in article after article well into the late twentieth century. Neither Beers nor Pelletreau make mention of Sybil's ride.

In 1907, Willis Fletcher Johnson listed Sybil's husband incorrectly as *Edward* Ogden and didn't include any biographical information on him. There was no mention of *Edward's* side of the family, but Johnson did mention that there had been an error in the reporting of the name in some previous publications. He notes: "Of these it is further recorded in the same register [he was referring to the register in a ledger kept by Colonel Ludington] that Sybil was married to Edward Ogden (the name is elsewhere given as Edmund or Henry Ogden)." [29]

In a later paragraph about Sybil, Johnson says: "Sybil Ludington, Colonel Ludington's oldest daughter, who married Henry Ogden, a lawyer of Catskill, N.Y. (elsewhere called Edward and Edmund) went to live at Unadilla, N.Y., and bore four sons and two daughters." It is no wonder researchers were confused.[30] Johnson wasn't even consistent in his own book with Edmond's name.

Both Sybil and her father were buried in the Presbyterian cemetery in Patterson, New York, beside Abigail Ludington, Sybil's mother. If Johnson had visited the Colonel's grave, he would have noticed Sybil's headstone, next to her father's. It reads:

IN
Memory of
SIBBEL
LUDINGTON
Wife of
Edmond Ogden
WHO DIED
Feb. 26, 1839
E. 77 yrs. 10 mo. & 21 ds.

In 1925, Ethel Saltus Ludington in her *Ludington-Saltus Records* confused the issue further by incorrectly identifying Sybil's husband as *Edward* Ogden. *The Yearbook of the Dutchess County Historical Society* in 1940 was partly correct. It correctly listed Major Edmund A. Ogden as her grandson. But it incorrectly stated that she "married October 21, 1784, *Edward* Ogden, a lawyer of Catskill and left four sons and two daughters."

One of the most surprising pieces of information may be found in *Early Settlers of New York State: Their Ancestors and Descendants* by Janet Wethy Foley, Volume 2, 1934: "Sybil Ludington had but one child, Henry Ogden, and one of her grandsons, Major Edmund Ogden, a distinguished officer of the U.S. Army, died at Fort Riley, Aug. 3, 1855 of cholera. Statements contrary to the above have since been found to be incorrect." Foley was correct, but apparently no one paid attention. Articles continued to claim that she had six children, despite the fact that there are no records to support this.

After researchers in the 1930s realized that Sybil's husband was not named *Henry*, the confusion it caused was far greater than the simple changing of the name from Henry to Edmond or Edward. *Henry* was first described as Sybil's husband and biographical information on him was credited to his father, Edmond. When writers who used Pelletreau and Beers, or even the family memoirs, for information on Sybil's husband reported their findings, it was on Sybil's son Henry and not on her husband Edmond. Henry was the father of six children—four sons and two daughters.

Unfortunately, researchers who believed that Edmond had always been a New Yorker never looked in his Connecticut military records. If they had, they might have uncovered the letters in Sybil's pension file that led to some interesting information about the lives of Sybil and Edmond Ogden.

### *Sybil Ludington's Ride*
By Berton Braley

Listen, my children, and you shall hear
Of a lovely feminine Paul Revere
Who rode an equally famous ride
Through a different part of the countryside,
Where Sybil Ludington's name recalls
A ride as daring as that of Paul's.

In April, Seventeen Seventy-Seven,
A smoky glow in the eastern heaven
(A fiery herald of war and slaughter)
Came to the eyes of the Colonel's daughter.
"Danbury's burning," she cried aloud.
The Colonel answered, " 'Tis but a cloud,
A cloud reflecting the campfires' red,
So hush you, Sybil, and go to bed."

"I hear the sound of the cannon drumming"
" 'Tis only the wind in the treetops humming!
So go to bed, as a young lass ought,
And give the matter no further thought."
Young Sybil sighed as she turned to go,
"Still, Danbury's burning—that I know."

Sound of a horseman riding hard
Clatter of hoofs in the manoryard
Feet on the steps and a knock resounding
As a fist struck wood with a mighty pounding.
The doors flung open, a voice is heard,
"Danbury's burning—I rode with word;
Fully half of the town is gone
And the British—the British are coming on.
Send a messenger, get our men!"
His message finished the horseman then
Staggered wearily to a chair
And fell exhausted in slumber there.

The Colonel muttered, "And who, my friend,
Is the messenger I can send?
Your strength is spent and you cannot ride
And, then, you know not the countryside;
I cannot go for my duty's clear;
When my men come in they must find me here;
There's devil a man on the place tonight
To warn my troopers to come—and fight.
Then, who is my messenger to be?"
Said Sybil Ludington, "You have me."

"You!" said the Colonel, and grimly smiled,
"You! My daughter, you're just a child!"
" Child! " cried Sybil. "Why I'm sixteen!
My mind's alert and my senses keen,
I know where the trails and the roadways are
And I can gallop as fast and far
As any masculine rider can.
You want a messenger? I'm your man!"

The Colonel's heart was aglow with pride.
"Spoke like a soldier. Ride, girl, ride
Ride like the devil; ride like sin;
Summon my slumbering troopers in.
I know when duty is to be done
That I can depend on a Ludington!"

So over the trails to the towns and farms
Sybil delivered the call to arms.
Riding swiftly without a stop
Except to rap with a riding crop
On the soldiers' doors, with a sharp tattoo
And a high-pitched feminine halloo.
"Up! up there, soldier. You're needed, come!
The British are marching!" and then the drum
Of her horse's feet as she rode apace
To bring more men to the meeting place.

Sybil grew weary and faint and drowsing,
Her limbs were aching, but still she rode
Until she finished her task of rousing
Each sleeping soldier from his abode,
Showing her father, by work well done,
That he could depend on a Ludington.

Dawn in the skies with its tints of pearl
And the lass who rode in a soldier's stead
Turned home, only a tired girl
Thinking of breakfast and then of bed
With never a dream that her ride would be
A glorious legend of history;
Nor that posterity's hand would mark
Each trail she rode through the inky dark,
Each path to figure in song and story
As a splendid, glamorous path of glory—
To prove, as long as the ages run,
That "you can depend on a Ludington."

Such is the legend of Sybil's ride
To summon the men from the countryside
A true tale, making her title clear
As a lovely feminine Paul Revere!

## The Ride of Sibyl Ludington
by Marjorie Barstow Greenbie

Come and listen, good people, and you shall hear,
Of a girl who rode, like Paul Revere,
Long the borders of Connecticut and New York,
Where the Yankees stored rations of flour and pork.

We were ready to fight the Redcoats to the ground,
If they came from their ships stranded out on the sound,
They, in vain, thought to keep us from being free,
And to keep us in bondage from George 'cross the sea.

Colonel Ludington summoned his men and did say,
"Your winter service is over, not to need you I pray,
For we have new recruits who are willing and strong,
To keep the Hudson Highlands you've guarded so long."

"So take up your plough and lay by your guns,
Return to your homes, to your wives and your sons,
Give thanks to the Lord for this moment to seize,
To plant all your crops and to take your ease."

In Danbury now there is food, there is rum,
We've plenty to eat if the Redcoats should come,
There is flour, molasses and bacon in store,
To keep us as we fight them to Hell's own front door.

General Wooster at Ridgefield can stop them cold,
Give them nothing at all to have or to hold,
But at last, long sleep in Connecticut ground,
If those Redcoats should land from their ships on the sound.

Sibyl Ludington stood by her father's side,
Sixteen and lovely, the Colonel's own pride,
The eldest of twelve, she had to cook and sew, too,
And at home with her family had plenty to do.

But she often found time with the soldiers to spend,
To their joys and their sorrows a willing ear she did lend,
As they now were sent back to the homes whence they came,
She spoke to them all and called them by name.

Now Sibyl was everywhere cheering the men,
With news of their homes, their families and friends,
She gladdened their hearts with hot coffee and bread,
For the long journey home that she knew lay ahead.

That night in her room o'er a well-filled board,
She and her family gave thanks to the Lord,
For the family was safe; no Redcoats in sight,
And many fathers and sons were home safe that night.

When the rest of her family had gone to bed,
Sibyl at last could rest her tired head,
She lay 'neath the quilt, with her sister, at rest,
And peacefully dozed in the family nest.

She woke with a start at a crashing noise,
At the door below she heard her father's voice,
"The Redcoats in Danbury? Did I hear you right?"
Then she heard a man saying, "They surprised us tonight."

"The people are fleeing! The town is aflame!
I spread the alarm long the road as I came,"
Then the colonel was saying, "Go muster the men,
We must get them together, our country to defend."

Now Sibyl was standing by her father's side,
She saw that the man was too weary to ride,
"Let me go," she said, "to call the men out,
If I get there in time, then the Redcoats we'll rout."

Her father objected to this long hard ride,
Through country where British deserters might hide.
He knew of the danger and his manner was grave,
When at last his permission to Sibyl he gave.

While she dressed and made ready, he saddled her steed,
He kissed her goodbye and bade her God-speed,
He gave her a stick to knock at their doors,
She could sound the alarm without leaving her horse.

A murky, spring mist cloaked every star,
And red, to the eastward, dim and far,
The fires of Danbury gloomed on her sight,
As Sibyl rode into the soft April night.

But the air was sweet with fresh April smells,
And the voices of peepers like tiny, gold bells,
Made vibrant the night as she skirted the pond,
And searched for the path she knew lay beyond.

She got tangled awhile in briar and brush,
And bogged in a swamp where the grasses grew lush,
But she would save all the people from suffering harm,
So onward she struggled to spread the alarm.

Out of the forest, over hill and through vale,
She raced to Mahopac by way of Carmel,
Then around to Farmer's Mills and back she flew,
Through Stormville to her home. . .her brave journey was through.

Now Yankees were men not easily ruled,
By hearsay or panic they'd not be fooled,
So some of them acted a little too slow,
To pull on their boots and get ready to go.

"I've been roused too often for nothing," one said,
"Why should I leave a good, warm bed?"
"Who is it now that's raising a storm?"
"It's the Colonel's daughter Sibyl. . .she's sounding the alarm."

Forty miles through briars and swamps she has gone,
"So get up and get out. . .we march at dawn,"
They pulled on their clothes and they got on their gear,
Then joining their neighbors, gave Sibyl a cheer.

But she was too tired when she got back home,
To realize the worth of the deed she had done,
Four hundred men stood ready to fight,
Where Danbury lay charred in the dawn's early light.

General Tryon awoke in the bed of a Tory,
Mission accomplished, but without any glory,
'Midst the chaos and ruin of that fateful night,
His men all lay drunk; not ten fit to fight.

They had found the food for which they had come,
Bacon, molasses, flour and rum,
The molasses ran sticky in every gutter,
They swizzled the rum; burned the bacon and butter.

That's how it was, you all know the rest,
Ludington's men were now at their best.
They fell on the Redcoats. The Redcoats retreated,
Their pride in the dust and their plans defeated.

The Yankees harried their rear and then,
Ludington proudly marched forth his men,
To join General Wooster and without pity or plea,
They pushed all the Redcoats back to the sea.

In that year of seventeen seventy-seven,
The people rejoiced and they all thanked heaven,
That the land lay secure in the soft summer light,
And that Sibyl Ludington had ridden that night.

# Sybil and Edmond

SYBIL LUDINGTON did, in fact, marry Edmond Ogden. He was the sixth child of Humphrey Ogden and Hannah Bennett, who were married in Westport, Connecticut, on November 22, 1743.[31] Hannah was the daughter of Thomas Bennett and Mary Rowland.[32]

Humphrey and Hannah Ogden had 11 children, the first six born in Westport and the last five in Weston, Connecticut. Edmond was born on February 12, 1755, and baptized on July 23, 1755.[33]

At 21 years old, he enlisted as a sergeant in a Connecticut regiment and faithfully fulfilled his military duties. His service prompted Sybil, when she was 77 years old, to take advantage of a pension passed as an Act of Congress on July 4, 1836. The file may be found in the National Archives in Washington, D.C. (Pension Files, R7777, Ogden, Edmond; Sebal) and is an important primary source of information on the life of Sybil Ludington Ogden.

The file contains, among others, four important letters. In one, signed by Sybil herself, she affirms:

the said Cybal [crossed out and changed to Sybal] Ogden is the Widow of Edmond Ogden who was a Sergeant in the Army and also in the Navy of the United States in the Revolutionary War and that he the said Edmond Ogden Enlisted at Weston in Fairfield County in the State of Connecticut in the Month of April 1776 as a Sergeant in the Company Commanded by Capt. Albert Chapman in the

State of New York,
Otsego County,

Be it known that on this eighth day of September in the year Eighteen hundred and thirty eight personally appeared before me Hiram Skinner one of the Judges of the County Courts in and for the County of Otsego being Courts of record — the Widow Sybil Ogden a resident of the Town of Unadilla in Otsego County and State of New York aged seventy seven years last April who being first duly sworn according to Law doth on her Oath make the following Declaration in order to obtain the Benefit of the provision made by the Act of Congress passed the 4th day of July 1836 And also of the late Act of Congress passed for the Benefit of Certain Widows and for other purposes That the said Sybil Ogden is the Widow of Edmond Ogden who was a Sergeant in the Army and also in the Navey of the United States in the Revolutionary War viz — that he the said Edmond Ogden Enlisted at Weston in Fairfield County in the State of Connecticut in the Month of April in the year 1776 as a Sergeant in the Company Commanded by Capt. Albert Chapman in the Regiment Commanded by Colo. Elmore in the Connecticut line — that he Marched with said Company to Albany in the State of New York — thence with said Company and Regiment and under the said Officers he served in the Capacity of a Sergeant at the German Flatts at Forts Dayton Stanwicks and other places untill the expiration of s Term and some days over when he was discharged after having served over one year as aforesaid in the Northern Campaign he was discharged in the month of April 1777 —

She the said Widow also says that she is under the impression, that he her said Husband served 6 or 8 Months in the year 1778 in the Neighbourhood of Boston — but cannot recollect who the Officers were or how long he served in that year — but she does further Declare and say that She does very well recollect that he her said Husband did serve at sea on board of several vessels commissioned by Congress and particularly under the

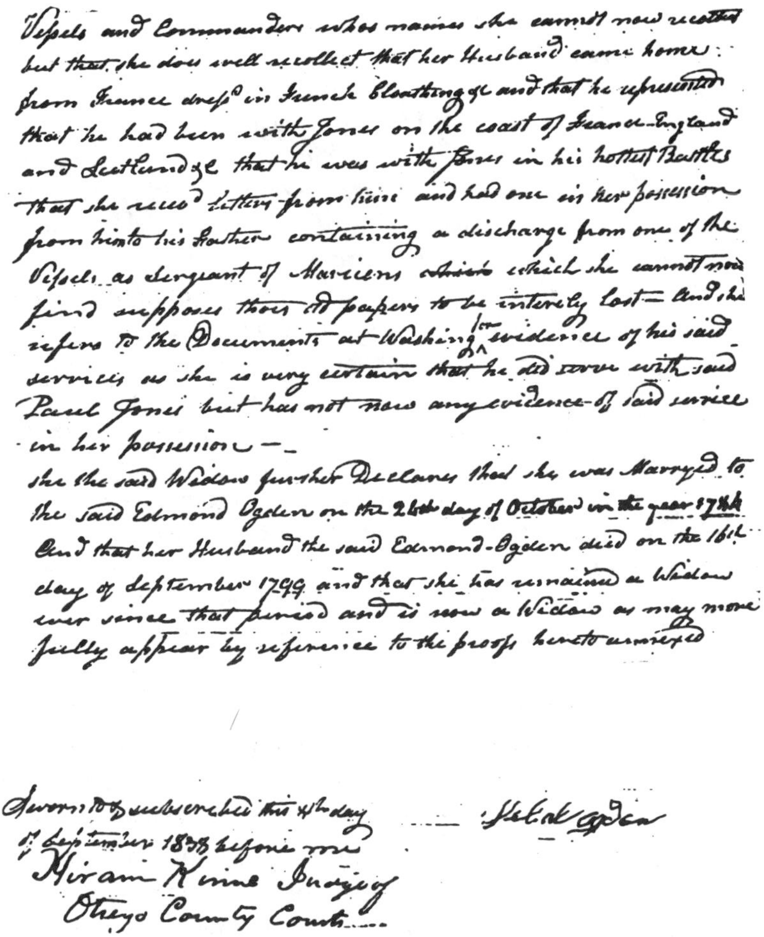

Vessels and Commanders whos names she cannot now recollect
but that she does well recollect that her Husband came home
from France dressd in French Cloathing &c and that he represented
that he had been with Jones on the coast of France England
and Scotland &c that he was with Jones in his hottest Battles
that she recd letters from him and had one in her possession
from him to his Father containing a discharge from one of the
Vessels as Sergeant of Mariens which which she cannot now
find supposes those old papers to be interely lost — And she
refers to the Documents at Washington for evidence of his said
services as she is very certain that he did serve with said
Paul Jones but has not now any evidence of said service
in her possession —
she the said Widow further Declares that she was Marryed to
the said Edmond Ogden on the 26th day of October in the year 1784
And that her Husband the said Edmond Ogden died on the 16th
day of September 1799 and that she has remained a Widow
ever since that period and is now a Widow as may more
fully appear by reference to the proofs hereto annexed

Sworn to & subscribed this 4th day
of September 1838 before me — Sibel Ogden
Hiram Kinne Judge of
Otsego County Court

**Letter of deposition signed by Sybil.**

Regiment Commanded by Col. Elmore in the Connecticut Line that he marched with said Company to Albany in the State of New York—thence with said Company and Regiment and under the said Officers he served in the Capacity of a Sergeant at the German Flats at Forts Dayton, Stanwix and other places untill the expiration of a term and some days over when he was discharged after having served over one year as aforesaid in the Northern Campaign he was discharged in the month of April 1777. She the said widow also says that she is under the impression that her said husband served 6 or 8 months in 1778 in the neighborhood of Boston but cannot recollect who the officers were or how long he served in that year—but does further declare and say that she does very well recollect that he her said husband did serve at sea on board several vessels, commissioned by Congress, and particularly under the command of Paul Jones in the "Bony Richard" [John Paul Jones and the *Bonhomme Richard*] and other Vessels and Commanders whose names she cannot now recollect but that she does well recollect that her Husband came home from France dressed in French Clothing and that he represented that he had been with Jones on the coast of France, England, and Scotland and that he was with Jones in his hottest battles and that she received letters from him and had one in her possession from him to his father containing a discharge from one of the vessels as Sergeant of Marines which she cannot now find and supposes to be lost.

It was through this file that some of Sybil's missing life story was finally revealed, and in a sense, enabled Sybil to tell her own story. Among other things, the file contained a deposition from Sybil's sister, Mary Gilbert, wife of Reverend Asahel Gilbert, signed by Bradford Winton, Judge of Probate for the "District aforesaid" and witnessed by Silas Haight, the Justice of the Peace of Dutchess County, dated August 21, 1838. In the letter, it was stated that Mrs. Gilbert

is a Sister of the Said Sebal Ogden, and the only Sister Surviving—that this deponent [Mrs. Gilbert] was personally present at the marriage of the Said Sebal Ogden, her Said sister, with the Said Edmond Ogden which marriage was solemnized before the Expirations of the Revolutionary war

*Facing page:*
**Mary Gilbert's letter of deposition. Mrs. Gilbert was Sybil's only surviving sister when the pension application was filed.**

State of New York } ss:
County of Dutchess }

Mary Gilbert of the Town of Poughkeepsie in said County, Wife of the Revd Asahel Gilbert, being duly Sworn, deposes & Says, that She is personally acquainted with Sibal Ogden, now a resident of the Town of Unadilla County of Otsego in said Widow, relict of One Edmund Ogden deceased, a revolutionary Officer, who Served in the Naval department of the United States of America Under Commodore John Paul Jones;— that this deponent is a Sister of the said Sibal Ogden, & the Only Sister Surviving;— that this deponent was personally present at the Marriage of the said Sibal Ogden, her said Sister, with the said Edmund Ogden which Marriage was Solemnized before the Expiration of the Revolutionary War, & Several years previous to the first day of January in the Year of Our Lord One thousand Seven hundred & Ninety four;— by the Reverend Eben Coles a regularly ordained & esteemed Clergyman of the Baptist Connection——

And this deponent further Says that Said Marriage occurred in the Town of Patterson, in the then County of Dutchess, now Putnam, in the State of New York — And further that the said Sibal Ogden widow as aforesaid of Said Edmund Ogden is, & has remained a widow ever Since the death of the Said Edmund, who died of the Yellow fever in the City of New York many Years ago, since the Year 1800, but in what precise Year this deponent knows not And further that the Said Sibal is aged & in very precarious health — Further this deponent Saith not

Subscribed & Sworn this
21st day August
A.D. 1838. Before me                     her
                                 Mary ✕ Gilbert
                                        Mark
Silas E Haight
Justice of the Peace in and
for Dutchess County —

State of New York } ss
Dutchess County } This may

and several years previous to the first day of January in the Year of Our Lord One Thousand Seven Hundred and Ninety-Four by the Reverend Ebenezer Cole a Regularly ordained and Esteemed Clergyman at the Baptist Connection. And the deponent further Says that Said marriage occurred in the Town of Patterson in the then County of Dutchess, now Putnam in New York." [Note that Sybil's sister missed their correct wedding date by exactly ten years. When Donald Lines Jacobus quoted Mrs. Gilbert's letter, he omitted the wedding date.][34]

A third letter in the pension files comes from Fanton Beers, then aged "Eighty-two years and over," whose testimony strongly supported Sybil's:

I was a Soldier in the War of the Revolution. That on the fifteenth day of April 1776 I enlisted for twelve months in a Company of I think Connecticut State Troops under the Command of Albert Chapman of Fairfield Town and County and State aforesaid as Capt. In Col. Elmore's Regiment and Marched with said Company to Albany where we joined the Regiment. The Regiment then marched to the German Flatts as called when we built the fort called Fort Dayton. We then marched to Fort Stanwicks where we relieved a Massachusetts Regiment and we continued and finished the fort by them begun and continued at said Fort under the command of said officers untill the 18th day of April 1777 at which time the Regiment was discharged making my time of service one Year and three days—I well remember Edmond Ogden then of Said Town and County of Fairfield and State of aforesaid Enlisting with me into said Company under Said Chapman in Said Col. Elmoe's Regiment and went to Albany with me and from there to the German Flatts and from there to Fort Stanwicks and continued there with said Company the full term of one year and three days and was discharged when I was. The said Edmond Ogden enlisted and Served as Sergeant of said Company the whole term aforesaid. He and I were Scholl boys and always

& State of Connecticut of Eighty two Years of age & over testify & say that I was a Soldier in the War of the Revolution. That on the fifteenth day of April 1776 I enlisted for twelve months into a Company of I think Connecticut State Troops under the Command of Albert Chapman of Fairfield Town & County & State aforesaid as Capt. in Col. Elmores Regiment and marched with said Company to Albany where we joined the Regiment. The Regt. then marched to Fort Stanwicks to the German Flatts so called where we built a fort called Fort Dayton. We then marched to Fort Stanwicks where we relieved a Massachusetts Regiment & we continued and finished the fort by them begun & continued at said Fort under the command of said Officers untill the 18th day of April 1777 at which time the Regiment was discharged making my term of service one Year & three days. I well remember Edmond Ogden then of said Town & County of Fairfield & State aforesaid enlisting with me into said Company under said Capt. Chapman in said Col. Elmores Regiment & went to Albany with me & from thence to the German Flatts & from thence to Fort Stanwicks & continued there with said Company the full term of One Year & three day & was discharged when I was. The said Edmond Ogden enlisted and served as Sergeant of said Company the whole term aforesaid. He & I were School boys & always very intimate untill he moved into the State of New York. The reason why the Company staid over the term of enlistment was in consequence of waiting for a Relief guard

Fanton Beers

Fanton Beers' letter of deposition. Fanton was
Edmond's schoolmate from Connecticut.

very intimate untill he moved into the State of New York.
The reason why the company staid over the term of enlistment was in consequence of waiting for the relief guard——
signed

Fanton Beers

The fourth letter, a deposition taken from Sybil's daughter-
in-law, Julia Ogden, provides information relating to Sybil and
Edmond's later life. Much of the information may also be found
abridged in Donald Lines Jacobus' *Families of Old Fairfield*,
Volumes 1 and 2.

The letters indicate that Edmond and Sybil were not "childhood sweethearts" as many articles suggested. Edmond was
born and raised in Connecticut and may not have been any-
where near Sybil while she was growing up. He enlisted in
Weston, Fairfield County, Connecticut, in April 1776 and
served as a sergeant in Captain Albert Chapman's company and
Colonel Elmore's regiment. He served until April 1777—the
month of Sybil's ride. When he entered the service, Sybil was
15, but Edmond was already 21. After her ride, Sybil remained
with her parents until she was 23 and helped to raise her
brothers and sisters. Edmond was 29 when the Reverend Coles
married him and Sybil in the same church she attended with
her family and the same church she was later buried behind.

Little is written about Edmond or Sybil in the years before
their wedding. However, Johnson, in his memoirs, quotes a
passage from an advertisement placed by Colonel Henry Ludington in a local newspaper for land he owned in 1781 in the
eastern part of Dutchess County near his home. The passage
includes a note about Sybil and her sister. "It was one of the
perilous duties of his daughters Sibyl and Rebecca frequently
to ride thither on horseback, through the Great Swamp, to see
that all was well on the property."[35]

"After the war he [Colonel Ludington] disposed of that
land, as the following notice, in the *County Journal and Dutchess
and Ulster Farmers Register* of March 24, 1789 shows":

To Be Sold By The Subscriber:
A Farm of about 104 acres of land in Fredrickstown in the County of Dutchess lying on the east side of the Great Swamp near the place where David Akins formerly lived. There are about thirty tons of the best of English hay cut yearly on such place, and considerable more meadow hay may be made, a sufficient quantity of plow and timber land, a good bearing orchard of the best fruit, a large convenient new dwelling house and a stream of water running by the door. The place is well situated for a merchant or tavern keeper. Whoever should incline to purchase said place may have possession by the first of May next; the payments made as easy as possible and an indisputable title given for the same. For further particulars inquire of the subscriber *or Edmond Ogden who keeps a public house on the Premises* [the author's emphasis].
Henry Ludinton
March 9th, 1789

The advertisement suggests a second reason for Sybil's visits to the property—Edmond Ogden ran a "public house" there.

Although Sybil and Edmond were not "childhood" sweethearts, it does seem they courted on the land they eventually owned. Although Johnson claims that the land was sold to James Linsley of Connecticut, a deed showing that Sybil and Edmond owned the land is on file at the Dutchess County clerk's office. Johnson's description of the land coincides with the description in the deed:

The result of this advertisement was the sale of the farm in question to a man from the former home of the Ludingtons in Connecticut. This appears from a document in the possession of Mr. Patrick, the original of an agreement made on November 5, 1790, between Colonel Ludington and James Linsley, of Branford, Connecticut by which the former covenanted and agreed with the latter "to sell a certain farm scituate, lying and being in Fredericksburgh butted and bounded as follows adjoining Croton River on the west side

and on the south by Abijah Starr and Ebenezer Palmer and
on the north by P. Starr & Samuel Huggins. Containing
about one hundred and five acres."[36]

The Ogden family moved to the area in 1783; the Colonel
had acquired the land in 1781 and sold it in 1790. On her trips
to check out her father's land with Rebecca, Sybil encountered
Edmond. They were married in 1784.

On October 22, 1779, the state legislature empowered the
governor to appoint a commission to take possession of property formerly owned by royalists. The commissioners handled
the liquidation of real estate, and Sybil's father and Benjamin
Birdsall acquired 173 acres of land. In 1786, Henry became sole
owner of 104 acres of the land. In 1790, he sold the land to James
Linsley of Branford, Connecticut. Either Johnson was incorrect about the Linsley sale, or Edmond and Sybil purchased the
land after 1790 and sold it in 1793.

A deed identifying Edmond Ogden as a farmer and husband
of Sybil Ludington and connecting him to Col. Ludington's
104 acres may be found in the county clerk's office in Dutchess
County.[37]

> This indenture made the twenty-third day of April one
> thousand seven hundred and ninety three between ED-
> MOND OGDEN of Frederickstown [Frederickstown was
> known also as Fredericksburgh] and County of Dutchess and
> state of New York farmer and Sybil his wife of the first part
> and SAMUEL AUGUSTUS BARKER OF Frederickstown
> aforesaid farmer of the second part witnesseth that the said
> EDMOND OGDEN and SYBIL his wife for and in consid-
> eration of the sum of four hundred and eighty pounds money
> of the said State to them in hand paid by the said BARKER
> have and each of them hath granted bargained sold alliened
> enfeoffed and confirmed and by these do and each of them
> doth grant bargain sell alien enfeoff and confirm unto the said
> BARKER and to his heirs and assigns forever ALL that
> certain tract or parcel of Land scituate lying and being in

Frederickstown aforesaid being parcel of a farm of one hundred and seventy three Acres conveyed to BENJAMIN BIRDSALL and Henry LUDINTON by SAMUEL DODGE and JOHN HATHORN Commissioners of forfeiture for the middle district and Lately released to the said HENRY LUDINTON by ABIJAH STAR who purchased of the said BENJAMIN BIRDSALL by certain Deed of partition bearing day the 27th day of May 1786 containing one hundred and four Acres be the same more or less comprehending all the Lands which on the said partition fell to the share of the said HENRY LUDINTON which farm of one hundred and four Acres is intersected nearly in the middle by the road leading from Dover to Danbury and on which said farm is a dwelling house standing on the east side of the said road or highway as the same is divided in a certain deed made between HERMAN HOFMAN late Sheriff of the County of Dutchess aforesaid and a certain JACOBUS VAN NUYS dated the 8th day of July 1791.

In any case, Sybil and Edmond were not only *not* childhood sweethearts, but may not have lived near each other until about a year before they were married. They were married about two years before Henry was born. It would also appear that Edmond was, in addition to being a farmer, an innkeeper in a "public house," an occupation that drew him to the rapidly growing village of Catskill on the Hudson River in Greene County.

The idea of Edmond being an innkeeper is not a new one. In a *Daily Mail* article, dated February 3, 1978, Mabel Parker Smith, the only historian to capture Sybil's days in Catskill, quoted Imer Bellinger, a stepdaughter of a descendant of Colonel Ludington. Bellinger quoted an article by Herb Geller in the *Patent Trader* (Putnam County) on June 9, 1957. In his final paragraph, Geller wrote, "Sybil Ludington never again figured into great events. She married a man by the name of Ogden who kept a tavern near Route 22 around 1839. She is buried in a churchyard at the Presbyterian Church next to her father who died in 1817 and her mother Abigail who died in 1825."

Geller revealed his source to me as Miss Emma Jane Ludington, one of Sybil's descendants. He warned me that seeing her to verify the story would be impossible since Emma Jane passed on sometime around 1969 or 1970. He was incorrect about the time of Edmond's tavern days. Sources clearly indicate that Edmond was long dead by 1839, and Sybil was dead by Feb. 26, 1839. Geller and Emma Jane Ludington had the date wrong but were right about Edmond's occupation as a tavern keeper.

There is additional evidence that Sybil was still in Dutchess County in the late 1780s. A brief mention of her appears in "A Chronological History of the Presbyterian Church of Patterson-Pawling, New York" compiled by Reverend James B. M. Frost. On page 10, he lists the year 1789 and states: "Col. Henry Ludington was a trustee of the church. His eldest daughter, Sybil Ludington, and Lt. Col. Ferris were members of the congregation."

The census of 1790 found Sybil and Edmond in Fredericksburgh. They left before the next census was taken. In the Department of Commerce and Labor Bureau of the Census report, *Ogden, Edmund* is listed on page 81 as the head of his household with one other *free white male of 16 years and upward, including heads of family/one free white male under sixteen years/and one free white female including heads of family.*[38]

While it is not clear who the other "free white male" was living with Sybil and Edmond, it is clear that they only had one male child after seven years of marriage.

The paragraph of the deed below places Sybil and Edmond in Fredericksburgh within three months of a school subscription signed by Edmond in Catskill on August 23, 1793:

> BE it remembered that on this twenty third day of April in the year one thousand seven hundred and ninety three before me JOHN RAY one of the masters in Chancery for the State

of New York personally came EDMOND OGDEN and SYBIL his wife grantors in the within indenture named and the said EDMOND OGDEN acknowledges that he signed sealed and delivered the same as his Voluntary act and deed for the uses therein mentioned and the said Sybil his wife being examined by me privately and apart for her said husband acknowledged, that she signed, sealed and delivered the same as her Voluntary act and deed for the like uses without any fear, threat or compulsion of from or by her said husband and I having perused the same and finding no material erasure or interlinations therein except those noted do allow the same to be recorded—JOHN RAY

RECORDED this preceading Deed the 13th day of August 1793

BEEKMAN LIVINGSTON D. CLERK

# The Catskill Years

IN 1792, Sybil and Edmond moved to the village of Catskill on the western shore of the Hudson River, leaving behind the relative peace and quiet of Fredericksburgh. By 1795, Catskill was in a transition period, destined to become a bustling port town: "It had outgrown its infant beauty of untouched forest—like a growing child—the white winged sloops that sailed up the Catskill [Creek], the log cabins and log fences, the ox-teams and the wood-roads had something of beauty, but as time passed it grew ungainly, the roads in spring hub-deep with mud, the houses set here and there with little beauty or symmetry."[39] For some there was success, but for others, the dream of a new and easier life never came to fruition. By the late 1790s, Catskill and the Ogdens found themselves facing some difficult years ahead.

The most active area of development, The Landing, was situated along Catskill Creek to accommodate commercial traffic drawn to Catskill from western New York. The Landing was located at the foot of Jefferson Hill, below the emerging village where residents of the small community watched processions of farm wagons loaded with produce and livestock making their way to The Landing. Sybil and Edmond and their seven-year-old son, Henry, settled into an environment dominated by the port and its countless activities and diversions. Details of life for the Ogdens in Catskill are sketchy, but county records enable us to follow some of the events of their lives.

A first mention of the Ogdens in Catskill is in James D. Pinckney's *Reminiscences of Catskill*. Edmond was recorded as having subscribed to the academy building fund during the time young Henry was enrolled in a school at The Landing. Such subscriptions were the only means of raising money for a school building. Pinckney discusses the records of subscriptions in papers belonging to Stephen Day dated August 23, 1793: "for the purpose of raising the sum of four hundred pounds, to have an academy erected at The Landing, in said town of Catskill . . . which sum is to be divided into one hundred shares, computing each share at four pounds." The list of subscribers included "Edmond Ogden." When another subscription was solicited, on May 10, 1795, it was resolved that 120 shares be added. Once again, Edmond bought 2 shares.[40]

There has been some confusion about Edmond's line of work in Catskill. In some sources he was listed as a lawyer, but there is no evidence to support this. His name was not included in the *History Of Greene County* under "Attorneys of the Era." He had been mentioned in 1789 as a keeper of a "public house" in Johnson's memoirs of Colonel Ludington. It is likely that Edmond chose to live in The Landing to make use of his skills. The Ogdens obviously took advantage of this bustling neighborhood to earn their daily bread by catering to the laborers and businessmen who needed food and lodging.

The Ogdens endured as a family until the fall of 1799 when Edmond died, presumably from yellow fever. In her deposition seeking a widow's pension based on Edmond's military service, Sybil stated, that "Edmond Ogden died on the 16th day of September 1799." The papers were filed in 1838. At the same time, in another deposition, Mary Gilbert, who was Sybil's only surviving sister, stated that "the Said Sibal Ogden widow as aforesaid of Said Edmond Ogden, died of the Yellow Fever in the City of New York many years ago circa the year 1800." Julia Ogden, Sybil's daughter-in-law, also deposed that Edmond died in "the month of September 1799." This information establishes the vague outline of where and how Edmond died, but it is most unsatisfying. There is no death certificate, no will, and no grave. There was no record of his death in the

**In 1811, Lyman Hall built his home on the property he bought from Sybil Ludington Ogden. It is believed that the foundation was part of Sybil's home and tavern from in 1804 to 1810. The house still stands on the corner of Greene and Main in Catskill.**

city's Surrogate Court Office records, and his name is not listed in the New-York Historical Society's Archives of people who died of yellow fever at the turn of the nineteenth century. For an unknown reason, Edmond Ogden's death went unnoticed, which is a sad state of affairs for the man who served with John Paul Jones on the *Bonhomme Richard* and eventually wed our hero.

After Edmond's death, Sybil was not alone in The Landing. Her brothers Tertullus and Henry lived nearby. Tertullus was mentioned in an evocative passage revealing a slice of Catskill life from Henry Hill's *Recollections of an Octogenarian.*

> In the north part of the village were the stores of General Samuel Haight, Andrew Brosnaham, Jacob Klein, Major Hawley, Orrin Day, Benjamin Haxtun and John W. Strong. When Doctor Porter built his house beyond that occupied successively by Jesse Brush, William Brown and Amos Corn-

wall, it seemed as if he had gone quite out of the village.
Looking from his house east to the river, and south to the
Point, no building was in sight; and at the top of the hill the
old court house and jail, and Olcott's dwelling-house and
rope walk stood alone. Across the creek were the houses of
Major Cantine, Doctor Benton, and Peter Dubois. South of
the shipyard stood that celebrated edifice, the Stone Jug, and
large storehouses on the wharves. In or near the lower part
of Main Street were Judge Day, Lyman Hall, Joseph Graham
and Tertullus Ludington, with their stores, the Widow Ogden and her tavern. . . .[41]

Not until 1803 does Sybil's name appear again in Catskill
records when she applied for an innkeeper's license. That she
felt competent to undertake such an occupation strengthens the
possibility that she had had considerable experience keeping a
tavern. What she learned living with Edmond proved to be the
mainstay of her economy over the next period of her life. Sybil
was listed as an innkeeper in Catskill in 1803—the only female
among 23 others.

By 1804, when Henry was 18, Sybil bought property at the
corner of Greene and Main Streets. A deed in the Greene
County Clerk's office is dated May 4, 1804, "BETWEEN
Reuben Webster of the County of Litchfield and State of
Connecticut of the one part and Sibel Ogden Widow of the
Town of Catskill, County of Greene, State of New York of the
other part." The purchase price was "for and in consideration
of the sum of Seven hundred & thirty two dollars lawful money
of the State of New York to him in hand paid. . ."[42]

Mabel Parker Smith discussed Sybil's purchase in a *Daily
Mail* article on January 11, 1978: "By piecing together the
evidence of published references such as Beers and Henry Hill
with that of property transactions in Greene County land
records, it seems safe to assume that the Ogden tavern sign
swayed at the southwest corner of Main and Greene Streets for
about six years from the purchase of the land. Smith notes

further that there was "possibly an erection of a stone structure thereon." But, she continues, "Sybil Ogden did not serve the public in the present handsome brick residence now occupying the entire Main Street frontage of that corner property running back the length of the Greene block to Hill Street. That she 'improved' the land built on it during her tenure is implicit in the $2275 figure for which she sold this and slight additional land to Lyman Hall in 1810 compared with her own purchase price of $732 in 1804."[43]

Sybil's first year in business was marked by an outbreak of yellow fever. Catskill was hard hit, especially in The Landing, where Sybil's establishment was on Greene and Main. The sickness was all around, and her new venture was certainly hampered by it. Yet she persisted in the face of this adversity. She was a strong woman and held her world together amid chaos. Sybil outlasted the fever and persevered in her chosen profession. J. B. Beers discusses the epidemic in Catskill."

> Though for general healthfulness the reputation of this locality stands high, the village has on occasions been ravaged by epidemic diseases. The first of these was in 1803, when the yellow fever broke out and for a time raged with much fatality. The epidemic commenced in the month of August. The first two cases occurred on the tenth, the third and the fourth cases on the eleventh, and the fifth and sixth on the nineteenth. The first three cases were in one family. There were altogether 30 clearly marked cases, and ten or twelve doubtful ones. One third of them began in August, and the others in September. Eight persons died, six of whom were males.[44]

An 1804 medical report written about the epidemic on and around Greene Street in 1803 was titled " Remarks on the Origin and Progress of the Malignant Yellow Fever, as it appeared in the Village of Catskill, State of New York, during the Summer and Autumn of 1803: In a Letter from Benjamin W. Dwight to Eneas Monson, M.D. of New Haven, Connecticut." The letter opens with an important premise: that the commonly held belief that yellow fever was "never of domestic origin" was wrong.

> As much pains have been taken, in various newspaper publications, to persuade the people of this country that the yellow fever is never of domestic origin, but an imported disease, I have been induced to state to you some facts which appear to me to support the contrary.[45]

Some of the doctor's report was repeated and summarized in *The History of Greene County* by Beers:

> The disease appeared to be confined to that part of the village near the Hopenose, mainly on Greene Street. On this street there were then several houses, and on the lower end of it a few stores [Sybil's brother Tertullus owned one of these]. Two or three hundred barrels of herring had been stored in one of these buildings during the month of the preceding May. A slaughter yard was then in operation in the village. The effect of it was so marked that Dr. Croswell claimed that he could tell beforehand, from its condition and that of the sewer leading from it, in connection with the weather, whether the families living near it would be visited with the sickness or not. The water was said to produce diarrhea if freely used. The people lived very much crowded together, generally two to four families in each house. These facts indicated bad sanitary conditions, and to them were attributed the progress of the disease, if not its origin. . . . Till the present year, the greatest number of cases has occurred in places considerably remote from the wharves. The reason is obvious. In addition to the stagnant waters in the gutters, &c. as above-mentioned, not more than two years ago a slaughterhouse was opened near the middle of Main Street, a little east from the road. Here a large number of sheep and meat cattle were slaughtered during the summer season. All the offals were thrown into the yard, and lay there from season to season. After every rain, the water which proceeded from

this yard ran into the street, and there became either partially
or wholly stagnant. In the neighborhood of this sink of filth
and poison, it has, in several instances, been very sickly. Some
cases highly malignant have, at times, occurred. In one small
house in particular, so situated as to take more of the stench
than any other, Dr. Croswell informs me, that the number
of cases of severe sickness, during the existence of this evil,
among the several families who have resided in it, have been
very remarkable.[46]

In 1805, Sybil was faced with a new dilemma. "Ludington
research in Greene County turned up intriguing insights into
Sybil's involvement in the business world, as a widow, an
independent, emancipated woman neither sheltered nor dominated by a man. A woman alone, suddenly charged with
management of her family affairs, she seems to have been caught
up in one of the countless speculation and land development
schemes which threatened ruin in the young country early in
the last century."

Amos Eaton was linked to the "Widow Ogden" in an 1805
land investment scheme involving 84 acres of land in Kiskatom.
The land deal eventually resulted in Eaton's conviction for
roguery and a sentence to life at hard labor without clemency.
Eaton was released, however, after five years and went on to
become a pioneer in the teaching and popularization of the
natural sciences and the founder of Rensselaer Polytechnic
Institute, Troy, under sponsorship of Stephen Rensselaer.

With all she had to do to keep her tavern going, Sybil helped
see Henry through his education. He became "Henry Ogden,
Att. at law of Unadilla, Otsego County," and married Julia
Peck of Catskill. Henry was 24 years old when he married. His
first son, Edmund Augustus, named for his grandfather, was
born on February 20, 1811. After the birth, mother, father, son,
and grandmother were on their way up the Catskill Turnpike
to Unadilla, where Sybil continued to stand by her son for the
next 28 years of her life.

# The Unadilla Years

**T**HE CATSKILL TURNPIKE, built in the late 1790s, ran from Unadilla to Catskill, and while it first brought business to the Widow Ogden's tavern, in the end it was the path to a new life with Henry and Julia. Unadilla was a place to raise a family in peace and quiet, but it was also a dynamic young community in the rapidly growing area of central New York. In many ways, it was a return to the life Sybil had left behind in Fredericksburgh with her parents.

A description of Unadilla one year before their arrival was included in *The History of Otsego County, New York*:

> Unadilla rapidly increased in importance. . .a post-township in the extreme southern angle of Otsego County, thirty-four miles southwest of Cooperstown, and one hundred miles south of west of Albany. . . . The surface is hilly and uneven but along the stream that forms the boundaries, as also some smaller ones, the land is very good and productive. . . . There is a quarry of stones, used for grindstones. There are sixteen saw-mills, that prepare great quantities of lumber for the Baltimore market, descending the Susquehanna in rafts. Five grain-mills, an oil-mill, and some waterworks, besides five distilleries of whiskey. There is one Episcopal church and fourteen schoolhouses, in which school is kept part of the year. . . . The whole population is 1,426, with 116 senatorial electors, 344 taxable inhabitants, and $141,896 of taxable property.[48]

Ironically, Otsego County was once part of Tryon County, named for Colonial Governor William Tryon, the same man

who burned Danbury in 1777 forcing Sybil to muster her
father's troops against him. Sybil Ludington was not recognized as a hero in Otsego County. Her years there were spent
in almost complete obscurity as "the Widow Sybil Ogden," and
as "the mother of Henry Ogden, Att. at Law." There are no
headlines for her achievements, no plaques, and no roadside
markers. She is not even buried there; her body was returned
to Dutchess (now Putnam) County and buried beside her
parents behind the church she attended as a child.

The Catskill Turnpike was a well-traveled thoroughfare to
central New York according to the *Unadilla Times*, and it
remained so for a quarter of a century.[49] Two stages were kept
regularly on the road charging a fare of five cents per mile. A
stage left Catskill Wednesday morning and reached Unadilla
Friday night. It is likely that one Wednesday morning in 1811,
Sybil Ludington Ogden, with her son Henry, his wife Julia, and
their child, Edmund Augustus, boarded one of those coaches
and headed for Unadilla, an important market town and a
thriving inland port where a young attorney could make a
name for himself and rise to prominence.

Henry was quite the country-gentleman in the little town
at the end of the turnpike. In style, respect, and dignity, life for
the Ogdens bore many similarities to the life of the Fredericksburgh Ludingtons. Sybil helped to raise her siblings in
Fredericksburgh much the way she helped to raise six grandchildren in Unadilla and suffered with them the heartaches that
mothers and grandmothers know only too well. One of the
children, her granddaughter Mary, died at 15 years old.[50]

In her deposition to the military pension review board,
dated August 8, 1838, Julia Ogden deposed that she was, "personally well acquainted with the Widow Sibal Ogden of Unadilla—that she, the said Julia is Daughter-in Law to the said
Sibal Ogden that they have lived in the same house together
about thirty years past."[51] A further documentation of Sybil's
presence in Unadilla comes from Frances Whiting Halsey's *The*

*Pioneers of Unadilla Village 1784-1840.* The Ogdens are mentioned throughout the book, but in particular as part of a description of the village as quoted from an article in the *Unadilla Times:*

> Next was the law office of Henry Ogden, Esq., occupying the site on which afterwards was built by Rufus Mead the store now standing vacant. The office was moved down near the mills and altered into a dwelling. Next was the residence of Henry Ogden and Family, consisting of himself, his mother, his wife, four sons and two daughters, occupying the site of the present Episcopal rectory.[52]

For many years it was believed that the office building and the house the Ogden family had occupied had long been torn down, but both Henry Ogden's office building and his house were kept intact well into the late 1900s. Each was moved on logs to new locations. The office building became part of the William Sewell home. A feature of the rear of the house was a small Masonic symbol, evidently put there by Henry Ogden himself, an active Mason. The LeFever family, who owned the building, donated the wooden symbol to the Unadilla Masons.

Sybil's son and daughter-in-law had four sons and two daughters:

> Edmund Augustus was born in 1811; died in 1855 at Fort Riley Kansas.
> Richard lived in California after serving in the Army.
> Frederick also later resided in California.
> Henry A. died Aug. 30, 1853, and was buried Dec. 11, 1854.[53]
> Mary was born 1818 and died August 19, 1833.
> Emily was born 1820, died Oct. 9, 1841, and was buried July 26, 1849 (brought from Maryland).[54]

Edmund Augustus graduated from West Point and served the Army in the Black Hawk, Florida, and Mexican Wars. He died a respected brevet-major at Fort Reilly, Kansas, in 1855 and is buried in Unadilla (see sidebar). There is little known of the other five children: Richard, who later resided in California, served in the Army as a captain and assistant quartermaster.[55] His brother Frederick also made his home in California and died there. Mary was born in 1818 and died in Unadilla in 1833. Emily was the family's second loss; she died in Maryland in 1841.

Life for Henry was very active in Unadilla, and as stated earlier, bore a remarkable resemblance to the life of Henry Ludington. Henry was named for his grandfather much the way his son was named for *his* grandfather. Both Henrys were active in their respective churches: Henry Ogden was a member of St. Matthew's vestry for many years, and Henry Ludington served on the board of trustees for the Presbyterian Church of Patterson.[56] They both held public office and both men served in the New York State Assembly.[57] Henry Ogden was also an active member of the Masons and a member of the Susquehanna Bridge Company, created to serve Unadilla. He was one of his village's first trustees and became commissioner of schools in 1826 and again in 1830.[58] While Henry Ludington was associated with names like Washington and Rochembeau, Henry Ogden was associated with names like Gouverneur Kemble, Washington Irving, and James R. Paulding.[59]

In all, Sybil Ogden and her son, Henry, came a long way together from their days in Catskill. From the death of her husband Edmond, through unquestionably tough business years, and until the day her son died a successful businessman, husband, and father of six children, Sybil Ludington never left his side.

# EDMUND AUGUSTUS OGDEN

A STUDY OF SYBIL LUDINGTON'S LIFE would not be complete without mention of Edmund Augustus Ogden—himself a hero—who was cheated by history, also. While his grandmother was forgotten for more than 120 years, Edmund was honored at the time of his death and then forgotten.

Sybil was with her grandson from birth until the time he left to become a West Point cadet, and she had reason to be proud of his distinguished career in the Army. In his memoir, Johnson reprints Edmund's obituary from the *New York Observer*, October 18, 1855:*

Major Edmund A. Ogden, of the United States army...died of cholera at Fort Riley, Kansas Territory. . . . On graduating [from West Point], Edmund A. was attached as Brevet Second Lieutenant to the First Regiment of Infantry, then stationed at Prairie Du Chien. He was subsequently appointed a First Lieutenant in the Eighth Infantry, where he served until appointed a Captain in the Quartermaster's department, in which corps he remained until his death. He served with credit and distinction through the Black Hawk, Florida, and Mexican Wars, and was created a Major by brevet, for meritorious conduct in the last named of these wars. . . . For the last six years previous to last spring [1849 to 1855], Major Ogden was stationed at Fort Leavenworth, where he has rendered important service to the army in his capacity of Quartermaster. From this post he was ordered to California, and he removed with his family to New York with the expectation of embarking on the 20th of April last, when his orders were suddenly suspended, and he was sent back to assist in outfitting the expedition against the Sioux Indians. He was afterward charged with the arduous duty of erecting, within three months, barracks, quarters, and stables for a regiment of troops at Fort Riley—a point about 150 miles west of Leavenworth, and which he had himself selected as a suitable place for a government post, when stationed at Fort Leavenworth. This place was not settled, and was an almost perfect wilderness. He took with him about five hundred mechanics and laborers, with tools and provisions, and commenced his labors. In a new and unsettled country, so destitute of resources, many obstacles were encountered, but just as they were being overcome, and the buildings were progressing, cholera in its most fatal and frightful form, made its appearance among the men, from two to four of them dying every day. Far removed from home and kindred, and accustomed to depend on Major Ogden for the supply of their daily wants, they turned to him in despair for relief from the pestilence.

He labored among them night and day, nursing the sick and offering consolation to the dying. At last the heavy hand of death was laid upon him, and worn out with care, watching, and untiring labors, he fell victim to the disease whose ravages he had in vain attempted to stay. . . .

It is interesting to note the estimation in which Major Ogden was held at Fort Riley. Johnson quotes from an article in the *Kansas Herald*:

The death of Major Ogden left a deep gloom upon the spirits of all the men, which time does not obliterate. His tender solicitude for the spiritual and bodily welfare of those under him, his unceasing labors with the sick, and his forgetfulness of self in attendance upon others, until he was laid low, have endeared his memory to everyone there. And, as a token of affection, they are now engaged in erecting a fine monument which shall mark their appreciation of the departed. The monument, which will be of the native stone of the locality, is to be placed on one of the high promontories at Fort Riley, and can be seen from many a distant point by those approaching the place. [The plaque will say] Erected to the memory of BREVET MAJOR E. A. OGDEN, The founder of Fort Riley; a disinterested patriot and a generous friend; a refined gentleman; a devoted husband and father, and an exemplary Christian. Few men were more respected in their lives, or more lamented in their deaths. As much the victim of duty as of disease, he calmly closed a life, in the public, distinguished for integrity and faithfulness. . . .

The revered soldier was quickly forgotten, however. W. F. Pride tells of the fate of Edmund Ogden's monument in *The History of Fort Riley* (1926):**

The stone was of the kind used in the building of Fort Riley. In time, neither the government nor anyone else heeding it, cattle made it a rubbing post, vandals chipped pieces from it and scratched their names on it and it became a wreck.... Another shaft was afterward erected, much better than the original. ... This, too, was neglected—left a rubbing post for cattle after the wooden fence around it rotted down. . . In 1887, General James Forsyth, then Colonel of the 7th Cavalry, took command of Fort Riley. . . . He secured a small allowance from the quartermaster's department, with which, and some labor within his control, he had it repaired—scratches worked out and a permanent iron fence put around it.

And so it seems that Sybil's grandson was remembered in Kansas. He was buried in the Episcopalian churchyard in Unadilla only feet away from where he undoubtedly played as a child, beneath a headstone now weathered and difficult to read. The gravestone is the only memorial to him in Unadilla. Dedicated by his friends in Kansas, it reads:

To the Memory of
Major Edmund Augustus Ogden
of the U.S. Army
Born at Catskill, N.Y. 1811.
Died at Fort Riley Kansas Territory, August 3, 1855

The friends who were with him during the last years of his professional life and near him at his death have asked the privilege of raising this monument wherein to record their honor for him as a citizen and soldier, their love for him as a Christian and a man and to tell how faithful to the last he was to humanity, how true to all his obligations.

*Johnson, p. 222.   **W. F. Pride, *The History of Forty Riley*, 1926, pp. 87-90

information as contained in his (or his widow's) application for pen_
sion on file in this Bureau. *Edmund Ogden* *Rej. 7777*

| DATES OF ENLISTMENT OR APPOINTMENT. | LENGTH OF SERVICE. | RANK. | OFFICERS UNDER WHOM SERVICE WAS RENDERED. | | STATE. |
|---|---|---|---|---|---|
| | | | CAPTAIN. | COLONEL. | |
| *Apr. 1776* | *apr. 1777* | *Sgt* | *Albert Chapman* | *Elmore* | *Conn.* |
| *1778* | | | *was Boatswain on officers* | *Staled* | |
| *also served on the Bon Homme Richard under Paul Jones* | | | | | |
| *and on other vessels names not Staled* | | | | | |
| | | | | | |
| *The claim was rejected on the ground of insufficient proof of marriage* | | | | | |

Battles engaged in, _____

Residence of soldier at enlistment, *Enlisted at Weston Fairfield Co. Conn.*

Date of application for pension, *Sept 8 1838*

Residence at date of application, *Unadilla Otsego Co. N.Y.*

Age at date of application, *he was 77 or old apr 11 36.*

Remarks: *Soldier married at Putnam in the Dutchess Co.*
*New York Stat___ __ He died September 16 1799*
*in New York City. A daughter on land, Julia Ogden was living*
*at Unadilla N.Y. 1838.*

**Very respectfully,**

_____

317928.64m.IV-07                                        **Commissioner.**

**Sybil's rejection notice from the War Department.**

# Conclusions

PERHAPS THE GREATEST IRONY in Sybil's life story involves the pension application papers she submitted to the War Department in 1837. Today they are essential documents, enabling us to know more about her, but Sybil's request was rejected. She couldn't produce her marriage certificate and was therefore denied compensation for her husband's service to his country.

Sybil Ludington was a Revolutionary War hero who was little known for a deed that contributed to her country's history. But she was more. Sybil was a lady in a war and time when women were not remembered well, and she lived a life that should not be forgotten. She fended for herself when her husband died, raised a son against all odds, and stood by him as he became a man of prestige and honor—a lawyer, an assemblyman, and a father of six children—one a West Point graduate who later became a hero.

The Ludingtons and Ogdens of the eighteenth and nineteenth century are gone—but we can keep them from being forgotten. With new information on Sybil, we can give this extraordinary woman the place in history she rightly deserves. It is my hope this short biography will contribute to the fight for Sybil Ludington's right to be remembered for who she was in the time and place she lived and died.

# Notes

1 Jane McMahon, "Sybil Ludington has her day," *Reporter Dispatch,* March 26, 1975, p. A3. Sybil was the 35th woman to be honored on a U.S. Postage stamp.

2 Donald L. Ephlin, "The Girl Who Outrode Paul Revere," *Coronet,* November 1949, pp. 50-52.

3 William S. Pelletreau, *History of Putnam County, New York,* 1886, p. 691. Pelletreau also mentions here that the Ludington house in Branford was destroyed by fire on May 20, 1754. Rebecca and Anne, the Colonel's younger sisters, perished in the fire.

4 Willis Fletcher Johnson, *Colonel Henry Ludington: A Memoir,* 1907, p. 35. (Pelletreau, on page 691 of his *History of Putnam County,* also called Elisha "son of William 3d.")

5 Ibid. pp. 35-36.

6 *Dutchess County Historical Society Year Book,* Vol. 25, 1940, p. 80.

7 Louis S. Patrick, "Secret Service of the American Revolution," *The Connecticut Magazine.* Vol. 11, No. 2, 1907, p. 266. *See also:* Johnson, pp. 30-31.

8 Ibid., p. 267.

9 Ibid., p. 268.

10 Ibid., p. 268.

11 *Dutchess County Historical Society Year Book,* Vol. 30, 1945, p. 76.

12 Patrick, p. 274.

13 Johnson, p. 45.

14 Patrick, p. 269.

15 James R. Case, *Tryon's Raid,* 1927, p. 13.

16 Ibid., p. 16.

17 Lincoln Diamant, *Revolutionary Women in the War for American Independence,* 1998, pp. 67-68.

18 James Montgomery Bailey, *History of Danbury 1684-1896,* 1896, p. 68.

19  Ibid., pp. 68-69.

20  Case, p. 24.

21  Patrick (see sidebar on page 24).

22  Johnson, pp. 89-91.

23  George L. Rockwell, *The History of Ridgefield, Connecticut*, 1923, pp. 103-119.

24  Johnson, pp. 89-91.

25  *Putnam County Courier*, "Revolutionary War Service of Local People Cited at the Dedication of Markers," Sept. 14, 1934.

26  *Congressional Record*, "Remarks of Hon. R. Barry, of New York at Garden Party, National Woman's Party—Extension of Remarks of Hon. Barry of New York in House of Representatives, Monday, May 20, 1963." Appendix A3168.

27  Pelletreau, p. 692.

28  J. H. Beers, *Commemorative Biographical Record of the Counties of Putnam and Dutchess* 1897, p. 978.

29  Johnson, p. 45.

30  Johnson, p. 219.

31  Donald Lines Jacobus, *History and Genealogy of the Families of Old Fairfield*, Vol. 2, Part 2, 1932, p. 712.

32  Credit must be given here to Edward L Woodyard of Armonk, N.Y., who conducted a genealogical search of the Ogden family enabling me to search Connecticut records for Edmond Ogden.

33  Ogden children as listed in Jacobus, p. 713: Ann—born 11/2/1744, baptised 11/25—married 4/7/1762 to John Coley; Mary—born 4/3, baptised 4/26/1747—married 4/22/1770 to Nathan Sturges; Joseph—born 3/1, baptised 3/19/1749—married 10/3/71 to Rachel Daniels; Humphrey—born 2/21, baptised 2/24/1751; Sarah—born 1/24, baptised 2/4/1753—married 12/24/72 to Stephen Hurlbut; Edmund [*sic*]—born 2/12, baptised 3/2 1755, died in New York State 9/16/99; married at Patterson, Putnam County, N.Y. 24, Oct. 1784 (pension rec.) to Sybil, who was living in 1838 in Unadilla, Otsego County, N.Y.; Eunice—born 12/28/56, baptised 1/16/57—married 11/19/78 to Pinkney Beers; Nathan—baptised 1/15/1759—married 4/13/1780 to Hannah Goodsell; Hannah—baptised at Weston 7/27/1760; Elizabeth—baptised 2/26/1763; Rhoda—baptised Aug. 3, 1766.

34  Jacobus, Vol. 3, pp. 239-240.

35  Johnson, p. 206.

36  Johnson, pp. 206-207.

37  Ogden-Barker Deed, Dutchess County clerk's office, Liber 12, p. 62.

38  *Heads of Families at the First Census of the United States Taken in the Year 1790, New York*, 1908, p.81.

39  J. V. V. Vedder, *Historic Catskill*, 1922, p. 68.

40  James D. Pinckney, *Reminiscences of Catskill: Local Sketches*, 1868, p. 77.

41  Henry Hill, *Recollections of an Octogenarian*, 1884, p. 21.

42  Ogden-Barker Deed.

43  Mabel Parker Smith, a Greene County historian, wrote a series of four articles on Sybil Ludington Ogden, *The Catskill Daily Mail*, Jan. 9-11, 1978.

44  J. B. Beers, *History of Greene County, N.Y.*, 1884, p. 142.

45  Samuel Latham Mitchill, M.D. and Edward Miller M.D. *The Medical Repository and Review of American Publications on Medicine, Surgery, and the Auxiliary Branches of Science*, Second Hexade, Vol. II, 1805.

46  Beers, *History of Greene County*, p. 143.

47  Smith, Jan. 12, 1978.

48  *History of Otsego County, New York*, 1878, p. 335.

49  "Historical Unadilla 1855-1930," n.d., p. 28.

50  Gertrude A. Barber, *Deaths Taken From Otsego Herald and Western Advertiser and Freeman's Journal, Otsego County, New York, Newspapers From1795-1840*, Vol. I, 1932.

51  See Julia Ogden's letter in the Pension Application Files: "Edmond Ogden #R777."

52  Frances Whiting Halsey, *The Pioneers of Unadilla, 1784-1840*, 1902, p. 142.

53  Ibid., p. 173.

54  Shirley B. Goerlich, *At Rest in Unadilla*, 1987, p. 275.

55  *History of Otsego County, New York*, p. 335.

56  See St. Matthew's Church records at the church rectory.

57  *History of Otsego County*, p. 26.

58  The Minutes of the Corporation from 1828, Village of Unadilla, located in Unadilla Town Hall.

59  Pelletreau, p. 615.

# Reference Chart

| Facts | Sources* | Resources/Notes |
|---|---|---|
| Sybil's parents were both Luddingtons. Her father's father and her mother's father were brothers. Sybil's parents were first cousins. | *Colonel Henry Ludington: A Memoir.* Willis Fletcher Johnson, 1907 | United States Military Academy Library at West Point. |
| | | A photocopy of the memoir is kept in a green binder at the Carmel Records Department (historian's office). |
| Henry was among the first Luddingtons to drop the second "d" in his name. The name also appears in documents as "Ludenton." | *Ludington-Saltus Records.* Ethel Saltus Ludington, 1925, p. 152 | |
| In 1761, Sybil arrived with her parents in Fredericksburgh at Lot Number 6 of the Philipse Patent in New York State, where Henry operated a successful gristmill. Sybil lived with her parents in their house until her marriage in 1784. | *History of Putnam County.* William S. Pelletreau, 1886 | |
| The Ludingtons raised twelve children in Fredericksburgh: Sybil, born April 5, 1761; Rebecca, born 1763; Mary, born 1765; Archibald, born 1767; Henry, born 1769; Derick, born 1771; Tertullus, born 1773; Abigail, born 1776; Anna, born, 1778; Frederick, born 1782; Sophia, born 1784; Lewis, born June,1786 | | The names of the Ludington children were recorded in a ledger kept by the Colonel. See Johnson, p. 45. |
| Henry Ludington served his king as a Captain of the Fifth Company of the Second Battalion of the Fredericksburgh Regiment of Militia in Dutchess County. By 1776, however, he became a staunch revolutionary, prompting General Howe, the British commander, to offer a reward of 300 English guineas for Ludington "dead or alive." | | |

*See bibliography for complete entry

| Facts | Sources | Resources |
|---|---|---|
| Sybil (also spelled"Sibbell," "Sibyl," "Sibel" and "Sebal") was referred to as her father's "most vigilant and watchful companion. . .her constant care and thoughtfulness, combined with fortuitous circumstances, prevented the fruition of many an intrigue against his life and capture." | "The Secret Service of the American Revolution," *The Connecticut Magazine.* Louis S. Patrick Vol. 11, No. 2, 1907 271-272 | Generally available in libraries along the Connecticut border in Westchester and Putnam Counties. |
| Danbury, Connecticut, was raided and burned on April 27, 1777, by William Tryon, Royal Governor of New York, Major General of Loyalist Provincials, and commander of the Danbury expedition. His mission was to destroy the revolutionarys' supplies reported to be stored there. Tryon's troops from 20 transports and six war vessels embarked at Compo Point near Norwalk at approximately 4:00 P.M. on April 25. By Sunday, April 28, many had been killed or wounded. Nineteen dwelling houses, the meetinghouse of the New Danbury Society, and 22 stores and barns with all their contents were torched. | *History of New York During The Revolutionary War.* Thomas Jones, 1879 <br><br> *History of Danbury Connecticut 1684-1896.* James Montgomery Bailey, 1896, <br><br> *History of Connecticut.* G. H. Hollister. Vol. 2, 1855, 296-308 | Reed Memorial Library, Carmel, New York. (Due to its age and frail condition, pages cannot be photocopied.) |
| Included in the materials destroyed: "4,000 barrels of beef and pork; 100 large tierces of biscuits; 89 barrels of rice; 120 puncheons of rum; several large stores of wheat, oats and Indian corn. . .30 pipes of wine; 100 hogsheads of sugar; 50 dittos of molasses; 20 casks of coffee; 15 large casks filled with medicine of all kinds...." <br><br> The revolutionary dead included General David Wooster. <br><br> Benedict Arnold's horse was shot from under him. | *Tryon's Raid.* James R. Case, 1927, 27 | Connecticut accounts of Tryon's raid are accessible in libraries and historic houses along Tryon's route: Westport, Weston, Redding, Bethel, Danbury, Ridgefield, Wilton, and Norwalk. |

| Facts | Sources | Resource |
|---|---|---|
| Col. Ludington was called on to muster his men and come to the aid of revolutionary troops en route to Danbury. Sybil rode 40 miles through a rainy night to alert her father's troops, the Seventh Regiment Dutchess County Militia. | *Colonel Henry Ludington: A Memoir.* Willis Fletcher Johnson, 1907 | U.S.M.A. Library |
| | | See also: Dutchess County Historical Society in Poughkeepsie, New York. |
| | "The Secret Service of the American Revolution" *The Connecticut Magazine.* Louis S. Patrick, Vol. 11, No. 2, 1907, 273 | Map of Sybil's ride showing historic markers and the location of the Ludington Mill is available at the Putnam County Historian's office, in Brewster, New York. |
| Sybil was aware of the dangers she would face going out alone that night, including: army deserters, "Cowboys," "Skinners," and royalists. | *History of Putnam County.* William S. Pelletreau, 1886 | |
| Her ride resulted in the Colonel's being able to get to Ridgefield and aid in the battle that helped drive Tryon back to his ships. | *Ludington-Saltus Records.* Ethel Saltus Ludington, 1925 | Road markers denote Sybil's route, Colonel Ludington's parade grounds, the former Ludington homesite, and the Colonel's route to Connecticut. |
| | *Old Dutchess Forever!* Henry Noble MacCracken, 1956 | |
| | "Signs to Mark Historic Ride of Revolutionary Heroine," Raymond H. Torrey. *New York Herald Tribune,* Sunday, Sept 17, 1934 | There are monuments, plaques, and museums throughout New York and Connecticut that commemorate the battles on the weekend of Sybil's ride. |
| | Keeler Tavern Museum pamphlets and brochures | Keeler Tavern Museum, 132 Main St., Ridgefield, Connecticut |

| Facts | Sources | Resources |
|-------|---------|-----------|
| In 1907, Sybil's ride was mentioned in a memoir by Willis Fletcher Johnson commissioned by family members. | *Colonel Henry Ludington: A Memoir*. Willis Fletcher Johnson, 1907, 219 | U.S.M.A. Library and the Kent Historical Society in Kent, New York. |
| Louis S. Patrick wrote an account of the ride in *Connecticut Magazine* in 1907. This is likely, the same person that Willis Fletcher Johnson credited as Lewis S. Patrick in his memoirs of the Colonel. Both men were known as thorough researchers of colonial American history. | "The Secret Service of the American Revolution," *Connecticut Magazine*. Louis S. Patrick, Vol. 11, No. 2, 1907, 273 | |
| While Willis Fletcher Johnson is said to be responsible for helping Sybil receive credit for her ride, Johnson clearly credits Patrick for "the collection of a large share of the data upon which this memoir of his ancestor is founded." | | |
| Inaccuracies by Johnson and others have made it difficult for later researchers to investigate Sybil's life beyond her ride. The most common confusion was with her husband's first name. | | |
| Researchers have long hoped that some mention of the ride before 1907 could be found in military records or family letters or diaries. As of 2000, no mention of the event has been discovered prior to 1907. | | |

| Facts | Sources | Resources |
|-------|---------|-----------|
| Sybil and Edmond Ogden were married on Oct. 24, 1784, in Patterson, N.Y. In a letter to the War Department, Sybil's sister, Mary Gilbert of Poughkeepsie, said she witnessed the wedding of the couple by Rev. Ebenezer Coles, Baptist Clergyman in Patterson, N.Y., Dutchess (now Putnam) County. Edmond was 29 years old and Sybil was 23. | Letter from Mrs. Gilbert in the National Archives (Pension Files R 7777) "Ogden, Edmond; Sebal"<br><br>*History and Genealogy of the Families of Old Fairfield.* Donald Lines Jacobus, 1932, 239 | National Archives and Records Administration, Washington, D.C. 20408 |
| Sybil's husband was incorrectly identified as Henry Ogden in Pelletreau's *History of Putnam County* in 1886. | *History of Putnam County.* William S. Pelletreau, 1886 | Generally available in Putnam County libraries. |
| In the Ludington memoirs by Johnson, Edmond was listed as "Edward (the name elsewhere given as Edmund or Henry)" and later in the same book as "Henry (elsewhere called Edward or Edmund)." | *Col. Henry Ludington: A Memoir.* Willis Fletcher Johnson, 1907 | Putnam County historian's office |
| J. H. Beers also mistakenly identified Henry as Sybil's husband in 1897. | | |
| A commonly repeated comment about Sybil's later life states that she married Edmond Ogden, "her childhood sweetheart." This first appeared in 1949. Edmond's military record, however, clearly shows him as having been a resident of Connecticut when he entered the service in 1776. | *Commemorative Biographical Record: Dutchess and Putnam Counties, N.Y.* J. H. Beers & Co. 1897, 978<br><br>"Girl Who Outrode Paul Revere," *Coronet Magazine.* Donald L. Ephlin, 1949 | Mahopac Library, Mahopac, New York and New York State Historical Association Library, Cooperstown, N.Y. |

| Facts | Sources | Resources |
|-------|---------|-----------|
| Sybil's husband was born in Connecticut and was living there at the time of her ride. His parents, Humphrey and Hannah Ogden moved to "Fredericksborough" in 1783– one year before Sybil and Edmond were married. | *History and Genealogy of the Families of Old Fairfield.* Donald Lines Jacobus, 1932, p. 239. | Maps and deeds located in the county clerk's office in Poughkeepsie, N.Y |
| Although there is no deed on record for the purchase of land in "Fredericksborough" for Humphrey Ogden Sr., there is a deed for the sale of land on June 7, 1887, "BETWEEN HUMPHRY OGDEN and HANNAH his wife and HUMPHREY OGDEN Junior all of Fredericksborough Precinct in Dutchess County and STATE OF NEW YORK of the one part and JOHN TOWNSEND of Oyster Bay in Queens County and State aforesaid of the other part." | *Index to Deeds-Dutchess County, N.Y.* Grantees 1757 -1785 Humphrey Ogden Jr., Liber 9, p.122, Grantor: William B. Alger<br><br>Dutchess County, 1785, Humphrey Ogden Jr. Liber 9, p.126<br><br>See also: Pelletreau's *History of Putnam County.* pp 639, 650, and 657 | |
| Several deeds listed for Humphrey Jr. and both "Humphrey Ogden Jr. of Fredericksburg" and "his father" are discussed by Pelletreau in a New York land transaction with John Townsend. (p.650). | Dutchess County, 1787, Humphrey Ogden Jr., Grantor Caleb Frisbie. Liber 10, p. 364<br><br>Dutchess County, 1788, Humphrey Ogden, Hannah, his wife and Henry Ogden Jr. of the first part, and John Townsend. Liber 10, pp. 384-5 | |
| There is also evidence that both Edmond and his father served in the Third Regiment of the New York Militia after their arrival in New York. | *New York in the Revolution as Colony and State.* James A. Roberts. Second Edition, 1898, 241-242. This edition contains a special notation as follows: "These records were discovered arranged and classified in 1895, 1896, 1897, and 1898." | |

| Facts | Sources | Resources |
|---|---|---|
| At the time of Sybil's ride, her future husband, Sergeant Edmond Ogden, had just returne. from a one-year tour of duty under Capt. Albert Chapman and Col. Elmore. He had enlisted at Weston, Fairfield County in April 1776 and served until April 18, 1777 (eight days before Sybil's famous ride). He served at German Flats, Fort Dayton, and Fort Stanwix. | Record of Service of Connecticut Men in the War of the Revolution. General Assembly, Hartford, 1889<br><br>Pension File #R 7777 Conn. Navy "Ogden, Edmond; Sebal." A summary of these records also appears in Jacobus, 1932 | A copy of the files are in the National Archives in New York City, 201 Varick Street, 12th floor, Northeastern Region M804. |

In 1778, he served an additional six to eight months in the Navy. He is recorded as having served at sea on board the "Bony Richard" [*Bonhomme Richard*] and other vessels.

Sybil's pension claim of 1837 was made when she was 76 years old. (Pensions "For Certain Widows" were granted by an act of Congress in July 1836.)

Sybil signed a letter of deposition for a pension application in September 1838. She died on Feb. 26, 1839.

Sybil's claim was denied because she could not produce her marriage certificate. Sybil signed a letter of deposition stating she married Edmond on October 24, 1764, but she did not attend the court hearing, "by reason of her age, bodily infirmities, and general disability." A copy of the claim rejection appears on page 76 of this book.

| Facts | Sources | Resources |
|---|---|---|

**Facts**

Edmond Ogden's parents were Hannah Bennett and Humphrey Ogden of Westport, Connecticut. They married at Westport, Nov. 22, 1743. (Hannah was the daughter of Thomas Bennett.) They had eleven children:

ANN - born 11/2/1744 baptized 11/25, married 4/7/1762 to John Coley

MARY - born 4/3/1747, baptized 4/26, married 4/22/1770 to Nathan Sturges

JOSEPH - born 3/1/1749, baptized 3/19, married 10/3/71 to Rachel Daniels

HUMPHREY - born 2/21/1751, baptized 2/24

SARAH - born 1/24/1753, baptized 2/4, married 12/24/72 to Stephen Hurlbut

EDMOND - born 2/12/1755, baptized 3/2, died in N.Y. State 9/16/99; married at Patterson, Putnam County, New York 24, Oct. 1784 (pension rec.), Sybil, who was living 1838 Unadilla, Otsego County, N.Y.

EUNICE - born 12/28/1756, baptized 1/16/57, married 11/19/78 to Pinkney Beers

NATHAN - baptized 1/15/1759, married 4/13/1780 to Hannah Goodsell

HANNAH - baptized at Weston 7/27/1760

ELIZABETH - baptized 2/26/1763

RHODA - baptized 8/ 3/1766

**Sources**

*History and Genealogy of the Families of Old Fairfield.* Donald Lines Jacobus, 1932, 712-713

*7,000 Hudson-Mohawk Valley (NY) Vital Records 1808-1850.* Fred Bowman and Thomas J. Lynch, 228

*8,000 More Vital Records of Eastern New York State 1804-1850.* Fred Q. Bowman, 1991

*Early Connecticut Marriages as found on Ancient Church Records Prior to 1800.* F. E. Bailey, 1968

**Resources**

Searching through the IGA North America Family Series at the Yorktown Family History Center of The Church of the Latter Day Saints, Rt.134 Yorktown Heights, N.Y., I found the address of Edward Lanyon Woodyard whose discovery of the Connecticut connection in the Edmond Ogden line was the key to finding new and important information about Sybil's life.

Important information about William B. Ogden may be found at the William B. Ogden Free Library in Walton, New York.

### Facts

In 1935, through the untiring efforts of the Enoch Crosby Chapter of the DAR, the New York State Department of Education, the Division of Highways, and the American Scenic and Historic Preservation Society, roadside markers were placed along the route that Sybil took on April 26, 1777. These markers sparked several articles and new interest in Sybil Ludington.

Many articles following the 1949 piece in *Coronet,* carry a standard paragraph about Sybil's life after her ride similar to this: "After her famous midnight ride, Sybil Ludington married Edmund Ogden who became a Catskill lawyer and was Sybil's childhood sweetheart. They had four sons and two daughters and moved to Unadilla, New York. One of her sons, Major Edmund Ogden, became a distinguished national military figure in the mid-1800s."

### Sources

"Revolutionary War Service of Local People Cited at the Dedication of Markers." *The Putnam County Courier Trader.* September 14, 1934

"Five Historic Roadside Markers Dedicated by D.A.R. Monday," *The Putnam County Courier.* May 17, 1935

Articles that include similar paragraphs about Sybil are listed in the bibliography at the end of this book and are discussed at length in the text.

### Resources

New York State Historical Association Library in Cooperstown, N.Y.

The *Patent Trader* in Cross River, N.Y. Libraries throughout Putnam and Dutchess Counties have files on Sybil Ludington with photographs and clippings that may be photocopied by patrons.

| Facts | Sources | Resources |
|---|---|---|
| In 1921, Rev. George Noble of Carmel, N.Y., wrote a poem in Sybil's honor. It did not attain the fame of Longfellow's poem about Paul Revere. Another poem, by Marjorie Barstow Greenbie in 1963, was set to music and presented at the unveiling of a statue of Sybil in the gardens of the National Women's Party at 144 Constitution Avenue, N.E., Washington, D.C. The poem was later read into the *Congressioal Record*. The song was made available by mail order on a 10-inch record. | *Poughkeepsie Journal*, April 28, 1975, includes a copy of Berton Braley's poem<br><br>*Congressional Record*, Appendix A3169, May 20, 1963, includes copy of Greenbie poem. | Copies of both Noble and Braley poems are in the "Sybil Ludington box" in Reed Library Carmel, N.Y., and in various libraries throughout Putnam, Westchester, and Dutchess Counties. |
| Much of the credit for Sybil's recognition as a hero is due to the efforts of the Enoch Crosby Chapter of the Daughters of the American Revolution (DAR), which has consistently fought for Sybil's right to have a place in America's history. | See bibliography for extensive list of articles on tributes paid to Sybil Ludington. | |
| An opera, poems, a statue, and a postage stamp are among the honors accorded Sybil. Students, who study her as part of New York State's curriculum on local history, write dozens of reports and poems on Sybil annually. | | |
| Unfortunately, many of the reports and poems by the children contain the same mistakes perpetuated for years by journalists and historians. | | |

| Facts | Sources | Resources |
|---|---|---|
| The DAR was instrumental in informing the public of Sybil's ride but included two errors in a magazine article published in 1949. Although they correctly identified Sybil's husband as Edmond, they incorrectly stated that Sybil had four sons and two daughters and that two of her sons became officers in the army--one of them E. A. Ogden. | "The Girl Who Outrode Paul Revere," Donald L. Ephlin, *Coronet*. November, 1949, 50-52<br><br>*Yearbook*: *Dutchess County Historical Society*, Vol. 30, 1945, 81 | |
| The Dutchess County Historical Society *Yearbook* for 1945 identified Sybil , also incorrectly, as the wife of a Catskill lawyer and mother of four sons and two daughters. | | |
| Although most articles claimed that she was the mother of six children, Sybil Ludington was the mother of only one child, Henry, who became a lawyer in Catskill and later moved to Unadilla. Henry fathered six children. The early mention of Henry as Sybil's husband confused researchers for years. | | |
| Janet Wethy Foley was the lone researcher to provide correct information. Others writing about Sybil ignored her 1934 piece. | *Early Settlers of New York State: Their Ancestors and Descendants, Janet Wethy Foley*. Vol. 2. Originally published serially: Vol. 1, 1934; Vol. 9, 1942. Reprinted in two volumes with added introduction, table of contents and indexes by Genealogical Publishing Co., Inc., 1993 | Carmel historian's office. |
| There is no evidence of birth records, death records, census records, or education records for any of Sybil's alleged children, except Henry. | | |

| Facts | Sources | Resources |
|-------|---------|-----------|
| Sybil and her husband are listed in a deed in Dutchess County for property formerly owned by her father. The deed is for the sale of property from Edmond Ogden of Fredericks Town and County of Dutchess and State of New York and Sybil his wife to Samuel Augustus Barker of Fredericks Town dated April 23, 1793. | Dutchess county clerk's office. Ogden-Barker Deed, Liber 12, p. 62 | |
| Sybil is listed in 1789 as a member of the congregation of the Presbyterian Church of Patterson-Pawling, New York. | "A Chronological History Of the Presbyterian Church of Patterson-Pawling, New York," Rev. Jim Frost, March 15, 1993. | Rev. Frost served at the Presbyterian Church of Pawling-Patterson for 30 years before becoming pastor in Saugerties, N.Y. |
| Edmond's name appears in an ad for the sale of land Colonel Ludington had acquired near Pawling. Johnson mentions trips to this property by Sybil and her sister Rebecca. It is likely that Sybil also visited Edmond on her trips and eventually settled there with him for the first few years of their marriage. | Colonel Henry Ludington: A Memoir. Willis Fletcher Johnson, 1907, 207 | |
| Sybil Ludington can be found in the 1790 census living with her husband, one male child "seven or under," and one male "white" adult. In this same census, Ludington is spelled Ludenton. | 1790 census for Dutchess County, No. 45,266, Fredericktown (taken on Jan. 3, 1791)<br><br>*Heads of Families at the First Census of teh United States Taken in the Year 1790.* | Yorktown Family History Center, Church of Latter Day Saints, Yorktown Heights, N.Y. |

| Facts | Sources | Resources |
|-------|---------|-----------|
| Edmond Ogden can be found in "Sketches of Catskill" as part of a document dated August 23, 1793 "for the purpose of raising the sum of Four hundred pounds, to have an academy erected at the Landing, in said town of Catskill." Edmond was listed as a contributor of two shares. At the time of the contribution, Henry was seven years old. Two years later, Edmond contributed again. | *Reminiscences of Catskill: Local Sketches.* James D. Pinckney, 1868 | Catskill Public Library. |
| | *Daily Mail.* Catskill, N.Y., Mabel Parker Smith, Mon. Feb. 3, 1978 | |
| There are no records of any legal transactions in Catskill that would indicate that Edmond had been a lawyer. | | |
| Beyond 1795, there is no evidence that Edmund lived in Catskill or anywhere. | | |
| Sybil is mentioned as a tavern owner in Beers: "The following were innkeepers in this town [Catskill] in 1803: Sibel Ogden. . ." | "Education-Innkeeper" *History of Greene County.* Beers, 1884, 121 | |
| In the Ogden-Webster deed of 1803, Sybil is listed as "widow." | | |
| Henry Hill refers to Sybil's tavern on page 19 in his *Recollections* when he writes about Catskill: "The Masonic brethren in their parades and marching made an imposing appearance. The lodge met in the chamber of Mrs. Ogden's tavern .. ." He mentions her again on page 21: "In or near the lower part of Main Street, were Judge Day, Lyman Hall, Joseph Graham and Tertullus Luddington, with their stores [Tertullus was Sybil's younger brother], the Widow Ogden and her tavern...." | *Recollections of an Octogenarian.* Henry Hill, 1884, 21 | |

| Facts | Sources | Resources |
|---|---|---|
| Sybil was widowed when Edmond died of yellow fever at 44. Sybil was 38, and Henry was 13. By the time Henry was 18, Sybil was in business for herself. Six years later, she sold the business for almost four times what she had paid for it, and her son was ready to be on his own. | Grantee Index M-R, 1800-1890, 583 *Index of Deeds.* Greene County, N.Y.

1804 Sybil Ogden/Reuben Webster

1810, Sybil Ogden and Henry Ogden/Lyman Hall Pension File #7777, "Ogden, Edmond; Sebal" | Catskill Public Library

Greene County's Clerk's office on the first floor of the courthouse in Catskill. |
| Catskill had an epidemic of yellow fever during 1803, when Sybil purchased of her tavern. Her husband's case of yellow fever was three years prior to the epidemic. | *The Medical Repository and Review of American Publications on Medicine, Surgery, and the Auxiliary Branches of Science.* Second Hexade, Vol. 2. Mitchill, New York, 1805.

"1803 Yellow Fever Made Catskill Famous: Treatment Strenuous But Some Survived" *The Daily Mail*, Mabel Parker Smith, 1981 | Articles on yellow fever by Mabel Parker Smith provided by her daughter, Barbara S. Rivette |
| Mabel Parker Smith stated that Sybil's tavern on Main and Greene Street in Catskill was known as Ogden's Corner. The property the tavern was on is well documented in land transaction records. Sybil paid $732 for the property and sold it for $2,750 only six years later. | Mabel Parker Smith, *Daily Mail*, January 11, 1978 | |

| Facts | Sources | Resources |
|---|---|---|
| Sybil was listed in a land transaction with her son Henry on August 1, 1810, for $237.20 with John and Gitty DuBois for lots 13 & 14, lying on the east side of Water Street and northwest side of Greene Street leading from "Ogden's corner" Westerly to the creek and bounded... | 1803, Sybil Ogden/Stephen Bayard<br><br>1810, John DuBois & Gitty DuBois/Sybil Ogden & Henry Ogden<br><br>1806, Sybil Ogden /Joseph Graham | County clerk's office, Catskill, New York. |
| Henry Ogden of Catskill married Julia Peck of Unadilla in 1810 in the Old Church of Catskill. | File in Vedder Memorial Research Library. Information was recorded on an index card in a box marked "church records," A verification of this was sent to me in letter form by Shirley McGrath of the Vedder research center. | Greene County Historical Society, Vedder Memorial Library and Research Center, RD 1, Coxsakie, New York. |
| Sybil's son, Henry Ogden was born in Dutchess County, became a prominent lawyer in Catskill, and later moved to Unadilla. He was a member of State Assembly in 1820, 43rd session. He reared a family of four sons and two daughters. His grave and the graves of his wife and four of his children are in a family plot in Unadilla. Two sons, Richard and Fredrick, are buried in California. | *History of Otsego County.* 1878<br><br><br>File on Richard Ogden in Washington, D.C. | New York State Historical Association Library, Cooperstown, N. Y. and the Putnam County historian's office.<br><br>U.S. Military records file in Washington Archives Center. |

| Facts | Sources | Resources |
|-------|---------|-----------|
| It is likely that Sybil took her son, her daughter-in-law, her infant grandson, and her $2,750 up the Catskill Turnpike to Unadilla to start a new life that continued for 30 years. Her son was active in law and politics. | Letter from Julia in the pension files. U.S. military records file in Washington, D.C. | Town Historian, and Village Historian, Unadilla, N.Y.

Unadilla Public Library. |
| Henry Ogden was as active a participant in his community as his grandfather, Colonel Ludington, had been: | | |
| Henry served on the vestry of St. Matthew's Church almost to the time of his death. | Curtis Noble, "The Records of St. Matthew's Church, Unadilla" | Records for St. Matthew's church. Rectory, Unadilla, N.Y. |
| He was an officer of the Unadilla Masons, Freedom Lodge No. 179.

In 1817, he was a member of the Susquehanna Bridge Company, created for the purpose of building a bridge across the Susquehanna River. | "The Beginnings of Masonry in Otsego County, N.Y." American Lodge of Research Transactions. Vol. 4, 1946-47 | The Chancellor Robert R. Livingston Masonic Library of Grand Lodge, 71 West 23rd Street, N.Y. |
| He was elected to the New York Assembly in 1820. | | |
| He was elected as one of Unadilla's first village trustees in 1828 with Isaac Hayes, Boswell Wright, Daniel Cone, and Johnson Wright | *The Village Beautiful.* Walter Hunt, 1957 | |
| He was a participant in the "Unadilla Hunt" also called, "The Oxford Chase." This group was known for its hunting expeditions and lavish parties. | *History of Otsego County.* 1878 | |
| Julia was a member of the Female Missionary Association of St. Matthew's Church as was her daughter, Emily. Mary Ogden died at 15, too young to have been in the Association. | Arnold B. Watson, "Records of the Female Missionary Association of St. Matthew's Church, Unadilla 1823." | |

| Facts | Sources | Resources |
|---|---|---|
| There are no known school records, church records or community service records for Sybil's grandsons, Richard, Frederick, or Edmund. | | U.S.M.A. Library/Special Collections at West Point.<br><br>*Index to Old Wars*: genealogy room of the New York Public Library in Manhattan. |
| Edmund Augustus Ogden was born to Henry and Julia on Feb. 20, 1811. | See U.S.M.A. files and handwritten letter from Henry stating Edmund's birth date. | |
| Edmund Augustus Ogden was a brevit major and assistant quartermaster, United States Army. He died with distinction at Fort Riley, Kansas, August 3, 1855, at 44. His widow is listed as Isabel. The couple had six children, and his family is said to have lived in New Haven, Conn., after Edmund Augustus' death. | West Point Register #649: *Biographical Register of the Officers and Graduates of the U.S. Military Academy at West Point, N.Y.* Bvt. Maj-Gen George W. Cullum, Third Edition, Vol. 1, Nos. 1 to 100. Boston: Houghton Mifflin and Co., 1891<br><br>*Index to Old Wars Pension Files 1815-1826*, Vol. 2, L-2, Transcribed by V. D. White, 822 | |
| | *New York Observer*, Thursday, Oct 18, 1855<br><br>"For Fort Riley" The Kansas Territorial Register, Saturday Morning, July 21, 1855<br><br>"Cholera at Fort Riley," *The Kansas Weekly Herald: Leavenworth Section*, James D. Pinckney. Saturday, August 11, 1855 | *New York Observer*: New York Public Library in its Annex. This article is the principal source used by Johnson in his book. E. A. Ogden is addressed in the "Later Generations" section of his book. |
| Edmund's brother, Richard Ludington Ogden, also served in the Army as a captain. N.Y. May 14, 1861 to May 14, 1864. | George E. Omer Jr. "An Army Hospital: From Dragoons to Rough Riders— Fort Riley 1853-1903" *Kansas Historical Quarterly*, Fort Riley, Kansas: Vol. XXXIII, Issue IV, Winter 1957 | Kansas State Historical Society, 6425 SW 6th Avenue, Topeka, Kansas 66615 |

| Facts | Sources | Resources |
|-------|---------|-----------|
| St. Matthew's Cemetery behind the Presbyterian church is the resting-place of Henry and his wife and four of his children. | *At Rest in Unadilla.* Shirley B. Goerlich, 1987 | St. Matthew's Church records. |
| Henry Ogden Esquire, died Nov. 27, 1837; Emily, died Oct. 9, 1841 (21yrs.old), buried in Unadilla, July 26, 1849 (brought from Maryland); Julia, wife of Henry Esquire, died Nov. 22, 1849 (58 yrs. old), buried, Jan.3, 1850; Mary, buried Aug. 21, 1833; Henry A., buried Dec. 11, 1854; Edmund Augustus, Major US Army, born Catskill, N.Y., Feb. 20, 1811 died Fort Riley, Kan., Aug. 8, 1855. Richard and Frederick lived in California and are not buried with the family. | Richard and Frederick were mentioned in *The History of Otsego County*<br><br>Deaths Taken from the *Otsego Herald and Western Advertiser* and *Freeman's Journal*, Otsego County, New York newspapers from 1795-1840, Vol. 1, Gertrude A. Barber, 1932<br><br>*Pioneers of Unadilla.* Frances Whiting Halsey. 1902 | |
| Sybil is not mentioned as having been a part of any group, organization, or event in Unadilla. | | |

# Bibliography

Amstel, Marsha. *Sybil Ludington's Midnight Ride*. Minneapolis: Carol Rhoda Books, 2000.

Bailey, James Montgomery. Compiled with additions by Susan Benedict Hill. *History of Danbury, Conn. 1684-1896*. New York: Burr Printing House, 1896.

Baily, F. E. *Early Connecticut Marriages*. Baltimore: Genealogical Publishing Co., 1968.

Barber, Gertrude A. *Death Notices Taken From the Otsego Herald and Western Advertiser and Freemans Journal. Otsego County, New York Newspapers*. Vol. 1, 1932.

Baumhart, Carl M. "The Teenager Who Outrode Paul Revere." *New York Herald Tribune*, July 17, 1960.

Beers, J. H. *Commemorative Biographical Record: Dutchess and Putnam Counties*. New York: J. B. Beers and Co., 1897.

Beers, J. B., ed. *History of Greene County*. New York: J. B. Beers and Co., 1884.

Bernstein, Paula. "A Legendary Woman Rides Onto A Stamp." *Daily News*, Mar. 20, 1975.

Berry, Erick. *Sybil Ludington's Ride*. New York: Viking Press, 1952.

Blake, William J. *The History of Putnam County, N.Y.* New York: Baker & Scribner, 1849.

Bowie, Jocelyn. "Putnam Will Give This Lady a Lift." *Reporter Dispatch*, White Plains, N.Y., Jan. 29, 1985.

Bowman, Fred Q. *8,000 More Vital Records of Eastern N.Y. State*. Rhinebeck, N. Y.: Kinship, 1991.

Braley, Berton, "Sybil Ludington's Ride." *The Sunday Star: This Week's Magazine*, Washington, D.C, April 14, 1940.

Brown, Drollene P. *Sybil Rides for Independence*. Niles, Ill.: Albert Whitman and Company, 1985.

Brutting, Margaret, et. al., eds. "An Historic Biographical Profile of the Town of Kent, Putnam County, N.Y." Town of Kent, N.Y.: New York Bicentennial Commission, 1976.

Carboni, Bob. *General William Tryon's Raid.* Wilton, CT: Wilton Historical Society Library, 1963.

Case, James R. *Tryon's Raid.* Danbury, Conn., 1927.

Clyne, Patricia Edwards. *Patriots in Petticoats.* New York: Dodd, Mead & Co. 1976.

Cobbs, Phyllis. "Putnam's Pride: Sybil Ludington and Enoch Crosby." *Patent Trader,* Bicentennial Edition, February 1, 1975.

*Congressional Record.* Appendix A3168. "Remarks of Hon. R. Barry, of New York at Garden Party, National Woman's Party—Extension of Remarks of Hon. Barry of New York in House of Representatives, Monday, May 20, 1963."

Cullum, George W. *Biographical Register of the Officers and Graduates of the U. S. Military Academy of West Point.* Vol. 1, Nos. 1 to 1000. Boston and New York: Houghton Mifflin, 1891.

Diamant, Lincoln, ed. *Revolutionary Women in the War for American Independence: A One-Volume Revised Edition of Elizabeth Ellet's 1848 Landmark Series.* Westport, Conn.: Praeger, 1998.

*Dutchess County Historical Society Yearbook.* Poughkeepsie, N.Y.: Dutchess County Historical Society, Vol. 25, 1940 and Vol. 30, 1945.

Engle, Paul. *Women in the Revolution.* Chicago: Follett Publishing Co., 1976.

Ephlin, Donald L. "The Girl Who Outroad Paul Revere." *Coronet,* November 1949.

"Five Historic Roadside Markers Dedicated by DAR Monday." *The Putnam County Courier,* Carmel, N.Y., May 17, 1935.

Foley, Janet Wethy. *Early Settlers of New York State: Their Ancestors and Descendants.* Originally published serially. Vol. 1, 1934; Vol. 9, 1942. Reprinted in two volumes. Baltimore: Genealogical Publishing Co., 1993.

Frost, Rev. Jim. "A Chronological History of the Presbyterian Church of Patterson-Pawling, N.Y." Patterson, N.Y.: The Presbyterian Society, 1993.

Gallt, J. A. *Dear Old Greene County.* Catskill, N.Y.: privately printed by the author, 1915.

Geller, Herb. "Sixteen-Year-Old Girl Rouses Militia to Fight British." *Patent Trader.* May 21, 1959.

_____. "Miss Ludington: Putnam Girl Paul Revere Influenced the Battle of 1777." *Patent Trader,* Vol. 45- No. 10, June 9, 1957.

Geller, Herbert F. *A Fight for Liberty.* Bridgeport, Conn.: The Post Publishing Co., 1976.

Goerlich, Shirley B. *At Rest in Unadilla*. Sidney, N.Y.: RSG Publishing, 1987.

Grant, Anne. *Danbury's Burning* . New York: Henry Z. Walck, Inc., 1976.

Green, Margaret Ludington. *Samuel Ludington: Ancestors and Descendents*. Smyrna, Tenn.: published by the author, 1968.

Greenbie, Marjorie B. "The Ride of Sybil Ludington." Washington, D.C.: *Congressional Record*, Appendix A3169, May 20, 1963.

Gross, Eric. "Sybil Statue Cured of Mouth Foam." *Putnam Courier-Trader*, June 14, 1989.

Hall, Marjory. *See the Red Sky*. Philadelphia: The Westminster Press, 1963.

Halsey, Frances Whiting. *The Old New York Frontier 1614-1800*. New York: Charles Scribner's Sons, 1917.

_____. *The Pioneers of Unadilla Village, 1784-1840*. Unadilla, N.Y.: St. Matthew's Chruch, 1902.

Haviland, J. C. "The Unsung Ride of Sybil Ludington." *North County News*, This Week Magazine Supplement, April 24, 1985.

*Heads of Families at First Census of the United States of America Taken in the Year 1790*. New York Heritage Series. Number I. Washington, D.C.: Government Printing Office, 1908.

Hill, Henry. *Recollections of an Octogenarian*. Boston: Lothrop and Co., 1884.

*History of Otsego County*. Philadelphia: Everts and Ferris, Press of J. B. Lippincott & Co., 1878.

"History Repeats Itself?" *The Putnam County Courier*, March 1965.

Hollister, Gideon Hiram. *History of Connecticut*. Vol. 2. New Haven, Conn.: Durrie and Peck, 1855.

Horne, Field. *The Greene County Catskills: A History*. Hensonville, N.Y.: Black Dome Press Corp., 1994.

Hunt, Walter L. *The Village Beautiful*. Unadilla, N.Y., 1957.

"Huntington statue ready for library ceremonies." *Danbury News Times*, Sept. 9, 1971.

Jacobus, Donald Lines. *History and Geneology of the Families of Old Fairfield*. Vol. 1; Vol. 2, Part 1; Vol. 2, Part 2; Vol. 3; 1932.

Jewell, Willitt C. *Putnam County in Southern New York*. New York: Lewis Historical Publishing Company, Inc., 1946.

Johnson, Willis Fletcher. *Colonel Henry Ludington: A Memoir*. New York: published by his grandchildren, Lavinia Elizabeth and Charles Henry Ludington, 1907.

Jones, Thomas. *History of New York During the Revolutionary War*. New York: New-York Historical Society, 1879. Reprinted by Arno Press, Inc., 1968.

*Kansas Historical Register.* "To Maj. A. E. Ogden for favors from Fort Riley." August 4, 1855.

Khasru, B. Z. "Famous Americans Meet at Fair," *Reporter Dispatch,* April 2, 1993.

_____. "Florida Woman Traces Her Roots to Putnam County War Heroine." *Reporter Dispatch,* February 25, 1995.

Kruk, Jonathan. "Sybil's Ride: A Fictional/Historic Account." *The Nimham Times Magazine,* March 1998.

Leroux, Marilyn. "Historic ride across putnam set to music." *Reporter Dispatch,* April 3, 1993.

"Living History Fair." *Reporter Dispatch,* April 2, 1993.

Ludington, Ethel Saltus, and Louis Effinghamde Forest, ed. *Ludington-Saltus Records* 1925.

MacCracken, Henry Noble. *Old Dutchess Forever!* New York: Hastings House, 1956.

Mahoney, Tom ."Night Riders of the American Revolution." *The American Legion Magazine.* June, 1972.

"Masonic History of Unadilla, N.Y." Unadilla: Press of the Times, 1902.

McDevitt, Robert F. *Connecticut Attacked: A British Viewpoint, Tryon's Raid on Danbury.* Chester, Conn.: Pequot Press, 1974.

McLaughlin, Tami. "Restaurant Salutes Sybil's Historic Run." *Patent Trader,* Sept. 21, 1983.

McMahon, Jane. "Sybil Ludington has her day." *Reporter Dispatch.* March 26, 1975.

McNamara, Tom. "U.S. Stamp to Honor Sybil Ludington." *Reporter Dispatch,* December 30, 1974.

Merkling, Frank. "Sybil Rides Again: Hear Her Story." *The News-Times Sunday Magazine,* March 21, 1993.

*The Midnight Ride of Sybil Ludington and The Mystery of the Statue of King George III and His Horse.* Wilton, Conn.: Pimpewaug Press, 1976.

Miller, Helen Coats. "A Portrait of Old Dutchess." *National Historic Magazine,* Vol. 77, 1943.

The Minutes of the Corporation from 1828, Village of Unadilla, N.Y., Unadilla Town Hall.

Mitchill, Samuel Latham, M.D., and Edward Miller, M.D. "Remarks on the Yellow Fever at Catskill, 1803." *Medical Repository,* Second Hexade, II, 1805.

Moore, James M. "The Night of the Fire." *Yankee,* April 1970.

Muscarella, Richard. "Sybil's Putnam ride alerted troops in American Revolution." *Putnam Courier Trader,* May 18, 1995.

Noble, Curtis. "The Records of St. Matthew's Church." Unadilla, N. Y., 1850.

"NOW Remembers Sybil, Putman's Paul Revere." *Patent Trader*, Dec. 17, 1972.

Ogden-Barker Deed, Dutchess County clerk's office, Liber 12.

Omer, George E. "An Army Hospital: From Dragoons to Rough Riders— Fort Riley 1853-1903." *Kansas Historical Quarterly*. Fort Riley, Kan. Vol. XXXIII, Issue IV, Winter 1957.

Patrick, Lewis S. *The Ludington Family, The First Name in America*. Marinette, Wis.: The Independent Press, 1886.

Patrick, Louis S. "Secret Service of the American Revolution." *The Connecticut Magazine*, Vol. 11, No. 2, 1907.

Pearlman, Skip. "Ludington Memorial Race Set." *ReporterDispatch*, Feb. 23, 1982.

Pelletreau, William S. *History of Putnam County, New York*. Philadelphia: W. W. Preston, 1886. Reprinted. Brewster, N.Y.: Landmarks Preservation Committee of Southeast Museum, 1975. Reprinted. Interlaken, N.Y.: Heart of the Lakes, 1988.

Pelton, Robert W. "The Midnight Ride of Sibyl Ludington." *New York Alive*. Vol. 9, Issue 2, March/April 1989.

Pension Application Files: "Edmond Ogden #R777." U.S. War Department. Sept. 8, 1838.

Pinckney, James D. *Reminiscences of Catskill: Local Sketches*. Catskill, N.Y.: J. B. Hall, 1868.

Pollak, Michael. "Heroine of 1777 Still All in a Revolutionary Lather." *New York Times*, Oct. 22, 1995.

*Record of Service of Connecticut Men in the War of the Revolution (Compiled by Authority of the General Assembly, Hartford)*, Hartford, Conn.,1889.

"Revolutionary War Service of Local People Cited at the Dedication of Road Markers." *The Putnam Courier Trader*, Sept. 14, 1934.

Roberts, James A. *New York in the Revolution as Colony and State*. Albany: Press of Brandow Printing Co., 1898

Rockwell, George L. *History of Ridgefield Connecticut*. Ridgefield, Conn.: published by the author, 1927.

Ross, Emily. "The Female Paul Revere." *Daughters of the American Revolution Magazine*. April 1967.

Sheperd, James. *William Ludington of Malden, Mass. and East Haven, Conn. And His Descendents*. Boston: The Press of David Clopp and Son, 1904 (reprinted from *The New England Historical and Genealogical Register* for January 1904).

Siegel, Suzie. "Teenage rider finally revered." *Tribune*, Tampa, Fl., Jan. 30, 1995.

Smith, Mabel Parker. "1803 Yellow Fever Made Catskill Famous: Treatment Strenuous But Some Survived." *The Daily Mail*, Catskill, N.Y., Part 1, Sept. 8, 1981.

_____. "Unsung Heroine of Revolution Became Inn-Keeper On Busy Main Street Corner In Early Catskill." *The Daily Mail*, Catskill, N.Y. Article in four parts, Jan. 9-12, 1978.

Thomas, Richard. "Sybil Ludington, Heroine: Who's Who on U.S. Stamps?" *Linns Stamp News*, May 8, 1989.

"A Tree Grows in Stormville." *Sunday New Yorker*, Poughkeepsie, Jan. 27, 1952.

"Sibyl Ludington's Ride Immortalized In Bronze." *Patent Trader*, Feb. 22, 1959.

"Spirit of 76." *Reporter Dispatch*, Mar. 25, 1975.

"Stamp Covers Offered." *Patent Trader*. Feb. 15, 1975.

"Sybil of the American Revolution." New York: Abigail Adams Smith Museum (playbill), April 1 and 4, 1993.

Torrey, Raymond H. "Signs to Mark Historic Ride of Revolutionary Heroine." *New York Herald Tribune*, Sept. 17, 1934.

Tower, Samuel. "Contributions to the Cause Stamps." *New York Times*, Mar. 16, 1975.

Townsend, Louise P. "Sybil Ludington: Revolutionary War Heroine." Enoch Crosby Chapter of the Daughters of the American Revolution. Dedication ceremony speech, June 3, 1961.

Vedder, J. V. V. *History of Greene County 1651-1800*. Catskill, N.Y.: County Historian, 1927.

_____. *Historic Catskill*. N.p. 1922

Warner, Fred C. "Heroine Rode Into The Night." *PatentTrader*, April 14, 1960

_____. "Sybil Ludington's Famous Ride." *PatentTrader*, April 20, 1960.

_____. "'Twas the 26th of April in 77 that famous ride—." *Patent Trader/Bicentennial*, February 1, 1975.

Watson, Arnold B. "Records of the Female Missionary Association of St. Matthew's Church, Unadilla 1823." Unadilla, N.Y.

Wical, Noel. "The Girl Who Outrode Paul Revere." *American Mercury*, 86:4143, Feb. 1958.

Winnick, Karen. *Sybil's Ride*. Honesdale, Penn.: Boyds Mills Press, 2000.

Wujcik, Gerald. "Sybil Ludington Statue Unveiled By Sculptress." *News Times*, Danbury, Conn. , June 5, 1961.